THE IRON HOUSE

THE IRON HOUSE

A Memoir of the
Chinese Democracy Movement
and the Tiananmen Massacre

MICHAEL S. DUKE

Introduction by
John G. Healey
Executive Director of
Amnesty International USA

PEREGRINE SMITH BOOKS

This is a Peregrine Smith Book,
published by Gibbs Smith, Publisher
P.O. Box 667, Layton, Utah 84041

Design by J. Scott Knudsen

Manufactured in the United States of America
93 92 91 90   6 5 4 3 2 1

**Library of Congress Cataloging-in-Publication
Data**

Duke, Michael S.
    The iron house : a memoir of the Chinese
democracy movement and the Tiananmen
massacre / Michael S. Duke.
        p. cm.
    Includes bibliographical references.
    ISBN 0-87905-255-4
    1. China—History—Tiananmen Square
Incident, 1989. I. Title.
DS779.32.D85   1989
951.05'8—dc20   89-29828
                CIP

The paper used in this publication meets the
minimum requirements of American National
Standard for Information Sciences—Permanence
of Paper for Printed Library materials, ANSI
Z39.48-1984 ∞

This book is dedicated to the living and the dead: to the memory of the courageous students, workers, and common people who gave their lives for democracy in China, and to the struggling people of Beijing who asked me to "tell the world what really happened."

CONTENTS

PREFACE

ICHAEL S. DUKE, ASSOCIATE PROFESSOR OF Chinese Literature at the University of British Columbia, Vancouver, witnessed the heroic 1989 Democracy Movement and the resulting massacre and purge in Beijing from the best possible vantage point: that of an expert in Chinese culture who was living on the Peking University campus at the time. Fluent in Chinese, he was able to interview protesters, record loudspeaker speeches, and translate the slogans, poems, analyses, and announcements on the "big-character" protest posters. He managed to work his way into the nerve center of the demonstrations, the headquarters of the Peking University Students Autonomous Association Broadcast Station, which had set up a "Free Speech Triangle" on campus served by loudspeakers.

He contributed financially to the cause of democracy and marched in protest demonstrations. Although he shrugged off the danger at the time, by doing this he risked arrest and jeopardized his ability to return to China. In the aftermath of the bloody crackdown of June 3-4, he interviewed victims and recorded names of some of the dead.

Professor Duke has extensive training in Chinese culture. He spent the entire 1986-87 academic year traveling about China with his wife, Josephine Chiu-Duke, living in Beijing and visiting 11 provinces and 22 cities. At that time, he solidified contacts with leading Chinese intellectuals and dissidents such as Liu Binyan, then the recognized conscience of the Chinese Communist party but shortly afterward expelled from the party and now in exile.

The author arrived in Beijing on May 18, 1989, on what was supposed to be a three-month visit sponsored by the United States Academy of Sciences. He was to interview writers and collect information for a study on the relationship between traditional Chinese culture and contemporary Chinese fiction—a field that gives him special insight into what was happening at Tiananmen.

On June 7 he was forced to cut short his trip because of the chaos resulting from the military repression of the democracy demonstrators.

Keeping his promise to those who dared to defy the corrupt government, he has written *The Iron House.*

Structurally the book consists of two parallel narratives braided together. There is both a personal memoir of Duke's experiences at Peking University, on Tiananmen Square, and elsewhere in Beijing, and a narrative history of the 1989 Democracy Movement and the Tiananmen Massacre. By weaving these two narratives together in this way until they meet in the savage slaughter of the innocents, he leads us toward an understanding of two sides of one historical event. On one side is the exhilaration and excitement of the Democracy Movement—the natural courage, naive hope, unbending dignity, and stoical anticipation of the students, workers, and common citizens of Beijing. On the other side is the Realpolitik of the Chinese Communist Party Central— the palace intrigues of the power struggle, the Machiavellian machinations, the cold-blooded calculations of cruelty, and the deliberate mendacity of a revolutionary gerontocracy. We hope that readers will come away with some sense of both the human drama and the historical significance of the terrible events that occurred in Beijing in the spring of 1989. And that they will want to join in some way the Chinese people's struggle for freedom and democracy.

Imagine an iron house without a single window and virtually indestructible, in which there are many people sleeping soundly. In a short time they will die of suffocation, but they will pass from slumber to annihilation without experiencing the sorrow of impending death. Now you shout out loudly, waking up a few of the relatively light sleepers, causing these unfortunate few to suffer the agony of irrevocable death. Do you really think you have done them a good turn?

-Lu Xun (1881–1936)

FOREWORD

OPES OF BETTER TIMES AND FOR NEW FREEDOMS rooted in justice, radiated last spring from Tiananmen Square in Beijing. Chinese citizens gathered in the square every day for seven weeks, peacefully demonstrating their belief that the time for change had finally come.

The poetry and prose, drawings and songs, essays and arguments flowing from Tiananmen Square reached every region of the world. Some sectors of the international community responded with enthusiasm and encouragement; some watched with trepidation. The free exchange of ideas in Tiananmen Square was itself an event of international significance.

The excitement both in China and abroad suddenly turned to horror on the night of June 3. Government troops attacked the peaceful protesters, turning Tiananmen Square into another of the world's infamous killing grounds.

The killing continued for six days. More than a thousand Chinese citizens died as troops fired on unarmed demonstrators and bystanders in Beijing. Thousands more were maimed. Soldiers spared neither children nor elderly men and women. The true death toll will never be known. The Chinese government threw a shroud of secrecy over the events of June 3-9. Yet eyewitness accounts and the bloodstains in Tiananmen Square attest to the atrocities committed.

The killing was not a spontaneous action or a consequence of uncontrollably escalating confrontation. Chinese authorities made a deliberate decision to "clear" Tiananmen Square of demonstrators through lethal force. Pro-democracy student protesters had been joined by teachers, workers, government employees, police, members of the armed forces, and other Chinese citizens. Their numbers had reached a million during May, turning the gathering into the largest popular demonstration of discontent in the history of the People's Republic of China.

The Chinese government attempted to justify the killing as a reasonable response to "counter-revolutionary rebellion" by a "tiny handful" of people exploiting student unrest. The stark truth is that the government used killing as a political tool to crush prospects for change.

Governmental policy of killing is not unique to China. During the year before the Tiananmen massacre, we saw similar events unfold in countries including Algeria, El Salvador, Israel and the Occupied Territories, Peru, Somalia, and Sri Lanka. Most of the victims were killed because of their opposition, or suspected opposition, to government authorities. Sometimes governments unleashed lethal force on citizens who merely associated with so-called political enemies.

Every killing ground in the world assaults the dignity of humankind and threatens the fundamental freedoms of all people. The world's governments pledged to respect basic human rights over forty years ago, in the aftermath of atrocities committed during World War II, by proclaiming the Universal Declaration of Human Rights. Freedom of expression, freedom of association, and freedom from torture and killing are rights that no government may legitimately deny its citizens. But many governments, fearing the free expression of ideas and peaceful demonstrations of political opposition, have trampled their human rights pledge with violence against unarmed citizens.

If the international community fails to hold any government responsible for protecting human rights, it gives tacit approval for violent oppression in other countries. If Chinese authorities can plan and conduct a massacre without becoming the focus of unrelenting international protest, authorities in other countries can anticipate similar impunity. For those who consider the events in Tiananmen Square as a remote and isolated tragedy, history offers a clear warning: The poisons of oppression are not contained within national boundaries. Look to your neighbors and to your own doorstep.

The Chinese government, like many other governments guilty of gross human rights violations, has lashed out at its critics abroad. It has denounced protests as interference with China's internal affairs. At the same time, the Chinese government continues to enjoy an active role in the international community and continues to participate in the deliberations of the United Nations and the U.N. Security Council. In other words, Chinese authorities want the advantages of international relations without the responsibility for upholding either international human rights law or the norms of human decency.

At the core of the issue, however, lies the well-established fact that universal human rights are, by definition, everyone's business. Humankind is linked by these rights, and responsibility for protecting them rests with all people. No matter where individuals live or what their political beliefs may be, everyone has the right and duty to call on Chinese authorities for an accounting of the Tiananmen Square killings.

Protest becomes increasingly urgent as news of the situation in China fades from the international media. The killing did not stop on June 9. Many thousands of Chinese citizens have been arrested in the wake of the massacre and subjected to summary trials in a format of "verdict first, trial second." Many citizens have been sentenced to death and executed solely because they attempted to exercise their basic human rights.

A Chinese government directive, known as Document No. 3, advised officials after the massacre to execute "counter-revolutionaries." The directive continues that the "number of executed and imprisoned people is not to be published" but that certain death sentences should be publicized "in order to make examples." In plain terms, the government is using terror to silence its citizens.

The spirit of peaceful protest cannot live today in Tiananmen Square. But if enough people throughout the world speak out, the commitment to basic freedoms spawned in Tiananmen Square may some day return there. We who can speak out must be caretakers of the spirit—for the sake of the dead in China, for those now imprisoned and tortured in China, and for the protection of our own human rights.

John G. Healey
Executive Director, Amnesty International USA
New York, December 1989

MAPS

BEIJING

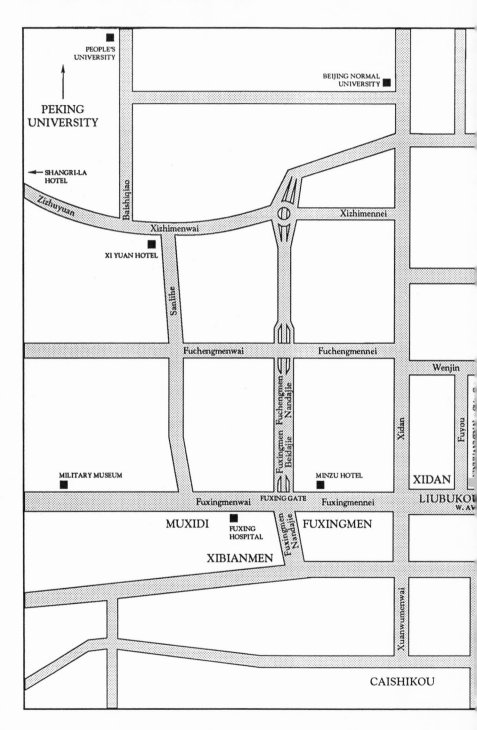

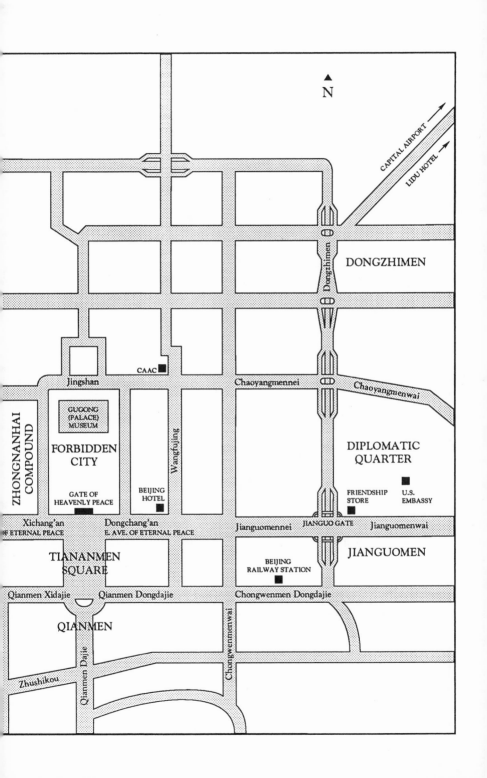

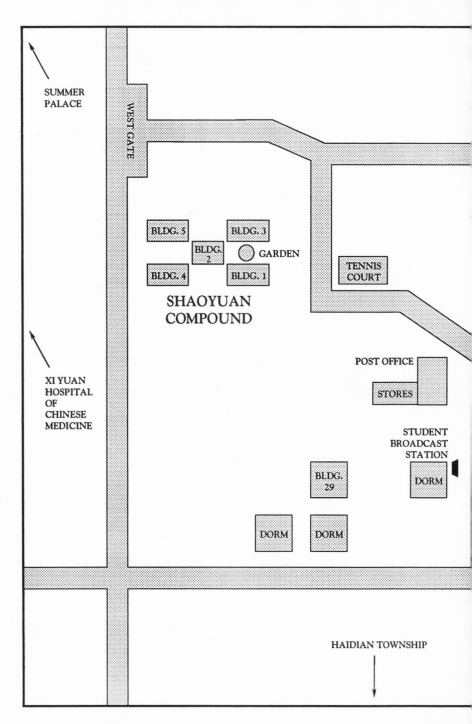

SUMMER
PALACE

WEST GATE

BLDG. 5

BLDG. 3

BLDG.
2

GARDEN

BLDG. 4

BLDG. 1

SHAOYUAN
COMPOUND

TENNIS
COURT

XI YUAN
HOSPITAL
OF
CHINESE
MEDICINE

POST OFFICE

STORES

STUDENT
BROADCAST
STATION

BLDG.
29

DORM

DORM

DORM

HAIDIAN TOWNSHIP

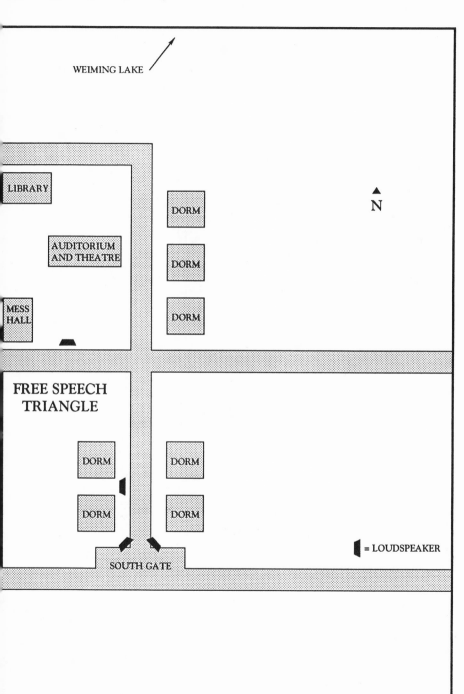

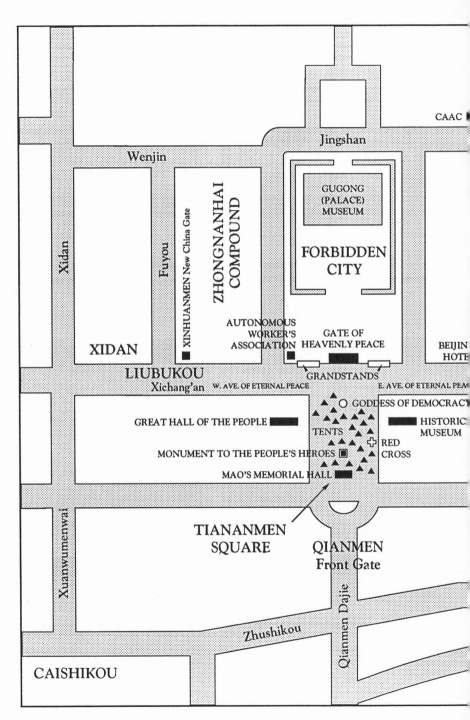

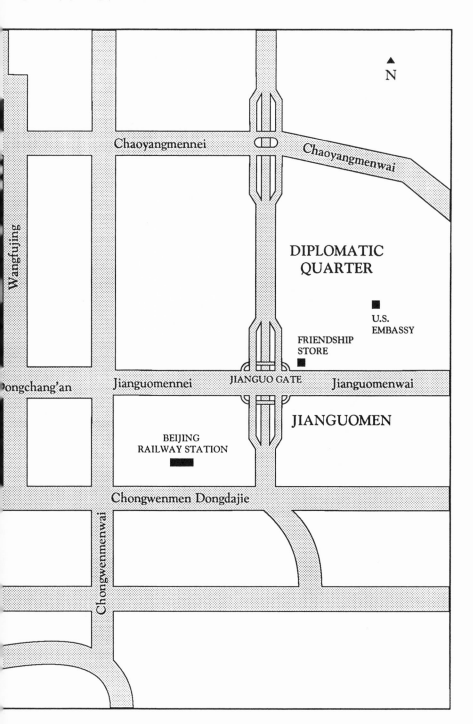

FREEDOM IN BEIJING

N MAY 19, MY SECOND DAY BACK IN BEIJING, I TOOK
a minibus to Tiananmen Square. Groups of people,
mostly students and young workers, were converging
on the square from all directions, pedaling bicycles,
and waving banners from factory trucks that were
supposed to be out hauling coal or bricks. I arrived at the square about
2 P.M. to find it full of people, about a million of them, walking around,
talking animatedly or just eating steamed bread stuffed with pickled
vegetables, bowls of noodles, purple and yellow popsicles, and drinking
China's ubiquitous orange pop. It was a wild, carnivalesque scene, as
if a country fair were being held in the middle of a great city. These
kids looked as poor as ever in their tattered shirts and dirty pants but,
unlike in 1986–87, they were happy. An infectious spirit of happy
chaos radiated from the enthusiastic crowd as they cheered on the
various small demonstrations that marched around the perimeter of
the square every few minutes. As devoid as the lives of Chinese youth
are in stimuli of any kind, I thought, this was really something to do,
something to be a part of.

It was a shock to return to China and see the people once again,
especially the young, as so many of them seemed graceless and crude.
In Vancouver, a friend from Taiwan who has never been to the
mainland commented that the first time she saw the students on
Canadian television they looked like bums, "no better than communist bandits." And by our standards, sometimes they do. Forty years
of communism and most of them still can't afford anything better. As
I watched them, I couldn't help but admire them for their struggle.
They were risking their university careers and future jobs, their only
chance to live a reasonable comfortable life, on the strength of their
courage and desire to give their country a better future.

They were brazenly flaunting huge banners reading, "DENG
XIAOPING STEP DOWN," referring to the 85-year-old chairman of

Tiananmen Square as I first saw it on May. 19.

the Central Military Commission (a post he resigned on November 9) and unofficial supreme ruler of China. After an hour of shoving in the sweltering heat, I could not even get close to the hunger strikers, pro-democracy students who were in an army tent on one of the higher levels of the Monument to the Revolutionary Martyrs. I walked around gathering impressions, breathing in this unprecedented air of freedom and gaiety in the usually drab, dull Beijing.

On a bus going toward the Beijing Zoo, the main transfer point for buses to Peking University, I borrowed a copy of that day's *Beijing Daily* from a woman sitting next to me. It was a wonder to read—there was more truth in that single edition than hundreds I'd read before. Most interesting was a lengthy report on dozens of public organizations, nearly all of them affiliated with the Communist Party, that were calling on their members and the general public to support the students. They included committees and organizations from schools, factories, government offices, restaurants and hotels, even the Communist Youth League of the Beijing Hotel. The groups urged the Politburo to meet with the students and devise ways to stop corruption and improve the economic and political system.

This was the newspaper that Peking University students had burned in front of a group of western journalists in December 1986, because of its lies. It was the same paper whose workers had carried a banner reading "The scapegoats are here" in a recent demonstration supporting the hunger strikers in Tiananmen Square—they were the scapegoats for the Propaganda Bureau, which forced them to write more lies about the students, and they were admitting it. This time there was honest reporting. The day was very hot and the ride took an hour and a half, but I was elated with everything I'd seen.

After dinner I returned to my room in Building Number Five at Peking University's Shaoyuan Guest House. This is a complex of five buildings, all of them five stories and without elevators or room service, that are used to house foreign experts, scholars and students. It was two years since my previous visit, and the place was even more beat up than before. Ninety percent of the evening news on Chinese Central Television (CCTV) concerned the Democracy Movement.

It reported that Li Peng, the hard-line conservative who took office as premier earlier in 1989, met with student leaders in the Great Hall of the People. Along with Education Minister Li Tieying and Beijing Mayor Chen Xitong, they were trying to "save" the students, the official media said, but the students refused their help. Student leaders Wang Dan and Wuer Kaixi refused to call off their hunger strike, saying this was not a true dialogue but only a meeting. They even scolded Li for being late and talking too much about irrelevant matters. On the television, Li Peng looked angry at the students for treating him as an equal, speaking frankly to him, and not agreeing to do what he said. He acted patronizing, telling them that his son was older than they, berated them, and ended the meeting by saying *Suan le,* forget it.

CCTV also said that before dawn that day, Zhao Ziyang and Li Peng had gone to Tiananmen Square. After Li left, it said, Zhao talked to the students. He asked them to go home, told them many things could be done to improve the system but everything was very complicated. He met with a cool reception and looked tired and sad, but did not display any of the arrogant anger that had shown in Li Peng's face. He looked like a man who was faced with a sadly impossible situation. The students should protect their health, go home, and trust the government to work on the proposals.

Weeping and declaring he had come too late, Zhao said good-bye. Later we learned that his final words to them were, "Fellow students, this is the last time I can meet with you."

Zhao, a former premier and the man supposedly next in line to succeed Deng, was the center of a great internal power struggle. Although we couldn't know it then, by this time he had already lost.

In other news, government officials were calling on the workers to keep at their jobs and not demonstrate and ruin the economy. The Ministry of Education urged primary and middle school students to stay in school and not go out supporting the university students in Tiananmen Square. The Chinese Red Cross called on government leaders to meet quickly with students.

Many other reports were broadcast about the students in the square, emphasizing their deteriorating health and the continued popular support for them, but the news did not list their actual demands: a direct dialogue with the government leaders who had real decision-making power; the right to form an independent student union; and a retraction of an editorial in the April 26 edition of *People's Daily* that had branded their movement a well-organized "disturbance."

The editorial was the official party line on the pro-democracy movement, and in effect, it accused the students of being the tools of a faction opposed to current party leadership. It denounced them as having ulterior motives opposed to the interests of the party and the nation—tantamount to criminal charges in China. This pronouncement had sparked the gigantic protests that resulted in the demonstrators occupying Tiananmen Square.

Dai Qing, an influential journalist from Beijing's *Guangming Daily*, attempted to negotiate with the students in Tiananmen Square on behalf of someone in the central government, presumably Zhao. Trying desperately to prevent the gap between the students and the government from widening further, she asked a writer, Zhang Langlang, to carry a message to the protesters that every possible compromise would be made to allow them to exit peacefully and honorably from the square. The government would promise to affirm the patriotic nature of the Democracy Movement, not take reprisals against the students, and openly negotiate with student leaders. But Zhang's efforts were unceremoniously rebuffed, as the students would not consider behind-the-scenes deals with people like Dai Qing, who had no official rank.

Late at night on May 19, Beijing was stunned to learn that Premier Li, President Yang Shangkun and Mayor Chen had declared martial law overnight, to begin at ten the next morning. The announcement was made at a special meeting of the Party Central and Beijing City political and military cadres, with keynote speeches by Li and Yang. The meeting was nationally televised, and Zhao was conspicuously absent.

As soon as martial law was declared, in the early morning hours of May 20, more than 110,000 soldiers from five provinces converged on Beijing from east, west, and south and attempted to enter the city. Then a near miracle occurred. Something completely spontaneous happened that was beyond the imagination of either the government or the students. Over 100,000 Beijing citizens swarmed out to block every road and bridge leading into the city and prevented the martial law troops from entering.

In the middle of the night, the BBC reported that the students had given up their hunger strike but were continuing a peaceful sit-in. Dai Qing was interviewed about the declaration of martial law. Speaking in emotional tones, she said a high-level power struggle was going on and was now being moved into the streets, as always happened during Mao's Cultural Revolution of 1966–76. "An irrational government is now confronted by an irrational people," she said.

Li Peng's and President Yang Shangkun's speeches were broadcast repeatedly on Chinese radio and television throughout the next day, May 20. They said martial law had been declared to end a "disturbance by a small group of people" that had made normal life in Beijing impossible. These people, they said, were trying to overthrow the Four Cardinal Principles and should be distinguished from the "patriotic" students.

Yang, the main speaker at the session, insisted, "Events to come will show you that it (martial law) is not aimed at the students."

I telephoned several Chinese friends about 9 A.M. One who had been active at Tiananmen told me not to come to his house now that martial law was declared. Another was afraid to even leave his home. Still another who had just returned from the square could only say he was exhausted and, "The situation is extremely bad, extremely bad."

At 10 A.M. martial law went into effect. One hour later, a news blackout was imposed.

After breakfast I walked to the Free Speech Triangle, the open area in front of the Peking University post office where student-run loudspeakers were broadcasting news and opinions. Directly in front of the post office and to its left were two long bulletin boards covered with big-character posters. Of varying length, all written in black characters, they contained an abundance of information: long analyses of China's political and economic situation; brief announcements of important events for the Democracy Movement; poems; satirical stories about the corruption and ignorance of the party leaders. Several were statements of support for the students, signed by prominent Peking University professors—up to 40 professors signed one poster. Hundreds of people stood around reading and discussing the posters. Most of them were students but there were also teachers, clerical workers and townspeople.

Peking University students have Spartan lives by western standards. They live in run-down dormitories near the post office on the south side of campus. They sleep under padded quilts in cold, dingy rooms with four to eight bunk beds and a few scattered wooden desks. There are many trees growing outside the buildings, but there is no grass, only hard, well trampled earth that roils up into great clouds of dust when the infamous Beijing winds blow throughout the cold winter months. Scattered around campus are large piles of coal used for heat in the winter and for cooking and heating water all year round. Coal dust blows in everywhere in the winter.

Three times each day—in the 90-degree summer or 20-degree cold of winter—all the students carry large metal bowls to the nearest mess hall to pick up their meals. They pay with paper and plastic coupons purchased at a distribution center on campus; that way, their meals are partially subsidized by the state. Each mess hall is furnished with long tables and a long sink so the students can wash their bowls in the cold running water. But most prefer to take their food back to their dorm rooms, and many finish eating on the move while heading back.

Today, as always, there were a great many walking from the nearby mess hall with their metal bowls, which looked like the sort of containers Americans use to feed their pets. The large bowls were piled high with three or four steamed buns, two regular bowls of white rice topped with two or three helpings of sauteed vegetables, or brimming with thick hot noodles. Instead of going back to their rooms to study, some students were stopping to read the latest posters and many more congregated under the window of the Student Broadcast Station, their most important source of information about the Democracy Movement.

The station operated from 8 A.M. to 10 or 11 P.M. It could be heard on five loudspeakers set up in trees just below the window in front of the station and directly in front of the nearby mess hall and auditorium, on a pole on the main street leading south out of campus, and on both

The South Gate of Peking University. Student Broadcast Station loudspeaker is on the left.

sides of South Gate, the main gate to the campus. There were always a few people gathered around these speakers. Nightly from about 8 P.M. on, large crowds that included many teachers, staff and their families, and nearby townspeople gathered there to listen to the "Free Speech Hours."

Anonymous critical essays would be read by the student broadcasters. Some students and professors who gave their names also spoke on theoretical issues of how to fight corruption and build democracy in China, or on the practical issues of strategy for the Democracy Movement.

Under martial law, all public gatherings like this were illegal and it was illegal for foreigners to be present at any such scene. Foreign journalists could not legally conduct interviews or photograph the gatherings. None of these restrictions had any effect on the people there or on me. I taped student broadcasts from 10 A.M. to 12:30 P.M. that day.

The students insisted that they would keep protesting and holding onto Tiananmen Square. They were forming picket groups, *jiuchadui*, which might also be translated as Public Order Brigades. Arming themselves with propaganda leaflets and the past week's newspapers, which were donated by the public, they were going out to the bridges and roads where the troop trucks were halted. There they intended to inform the soldiers of the true situation: there was no disturbance, they said, only a "Patriotic Democratic Movement." Many letters of support were read over the loudspeakers both from inside China and from Chinese students in the United States.

I decided it was time to buy a bicycle and get a better look at the city. At Haidian Township, across the street from campus, I haggled with *getihu* (private entrepreneurs) about the price of a secondhand bike. These fellows were as crafty and greedy as ever, but they were also friendly to a Chinese-speaking foreigner who obviously understood their game.

They too supported the students. As one said, "The more democracy and openness we have, the more money we can make." At first they tried to pawn off a broken-down old bike on me, one that wobbled like a drunkard when it got up a little speed. *Suan-le,* "Forget it," I said.

They looked at each other and laughed. "This dude's no sucker," a couple whispered to each other while a third went off to find a decent bike. "*Xianshen,* sir, how 'bout this one?" The second bike was a very serviceable Phoenix, made a smooth sound when it coasted, had good tires and a shiny original paint job.

"Not bad, how much? 160 *renminbi?* No way!" My hosts had told me a used bike ought to cost about 100 to 120 *yuan,* or *renminbi,* "people's money."

"I'll give you 100."

" *Xiao-hua,* you gotta be kidding. It's almost brand new."

I looked the bike over again slowly front to back and top to bottom. "A hundred and twenty and that's it. You want to sell it or what?"

"A hundred and twenty? Foreign exchange certificates? Make it FEC and it's a deal, OK?"

FEC dollars are what foreigners receive when they exchange money at the Bank of China. They are required for purchasing anything, including meals, at China's luxury hotels. Thus they are worth between 160 and 170 *yuan* per 100 FEC on the black market. The *getihu* are the black market in currency trades throughout China.

"FEC? OK, 110 FEC," I said. I pointed out that was more than the 160 *yuan* they originally asked.

"OK, OK, you're really terrible, but what can I do?" asked the *getihu*. "I need the FEC."

I paid the young man and then came the inevitable question, "Can you sell me some more FEC?"

"How much are you offering?"

"Hundred fifty to a hundred."

"Come on, that's the 1986 price," I said.

"Oh, ah, 160, OK?"

"Well, maybe next time."

"We'll be here every day."

"Right. If anything goes wrong with this bike, I'll be back to see you."

"No problem, *zaijian*, good-bye."

"*Zaijian*."

I probably paid too much for the bike—who knows where those fellows got it? But I always enjoy haggling with them. Don't get me wrong, though. I wouldn't bargain like that with poor shopkeepers or peasants selling fruit and vegetables—I always give them FEC at par—but those guys are rich. Down at "Jianguo Alley," the nickname my 1986–87 students gave to the free market just south of the American Embassy, they all have big bags full of money, RMB, FEC, and U.S. dollars. No wonder the middle-level party members were jealous.

Starting off on my first bicycle ride across Beijing, I felt a sense of exhilaration. I pedaled south from Peking University along Baishiqiao Road, going through Zhongguan Village and on past the Friendship Hotel. The names of all the streets in Beijing change every few blocks according to the district or a nearby historic landmark. Thus, at one point I turned east onto Fuxingmen Waijie, which means "Street Beyond the Fuxing [Restoration] Gate," but it's the same street as Changan Xijie, "West Avenue of Eternal Peace," which leads to Tiananmen from the west.

As I struggled to pedal up over the Fuxing Gate Overpass, the blue and white street sign said it was five kilometers (three miles) to Tiananmen, "The Gate of Heavenly Peace." I rode past several parks and a compound said to be reserved for heads of state. The ride was pleasant, but despite the construction of many new buildings, Beijing was even shabbier than when we lived there in 1986–87. Still, the open and friendly attitude of the people in this ancient capital was unlike anything I'd encountered before.

Many groups of cyclists were heading toward the square. I talked with three young men as we rode down Sanlihe Road. They were glad to meet and talk to a foreigner, especially one who claimed to be a visiting scholar at the Peking University Department of Chinese Literature. I wore a red and gold badge pinned to my red and white baseball cap, with the words *Beijing Daxue*, Peking University, on it.

They told of their disgust with the government's corruption and their hope that the students' demands would eventually be addressed in a dialogue, even if not met right away. They worked in an office now but had attended universities a few years before. Everyone their age at the office had visited the square to support the students. Asked what the party leaders at their office thought, they said they either actively supported the students or closed their eyes to the pro-democracy activism of other people.

I had innumerable short conversations of this type during my stay in Beijing. Just a few cab drivers were indifferent to the demonstrations, and even they grumbled about the government's stupidity. Only some middle-level party officials were openly opposed to the students.

As I approached Xinhuamen, the "New China Gate" about a mile west of Tiananmen Square, traffic became quite congested. Behind the intersection are two nerve centers of the government, the head-quarters of the Chinese Communist Party Central and the compound called Zhongnanhai, "South Central Lake." Zhongnanhai is where Deng, Zhao and other high-level Communist Party leaders sometimes live.

A large crowd was milling around in front of and across from New China Gate, with many students and workers staging a sit-in demonstration. A favorite place for delivery trucks to park and sell newspapers was across the street from Xinhuamen. There were also lengthy posters at the intersection and on huge billboards that had been intended to advertise industrial products.

I stopped to read many of them into my tape recorder, and collected a small crowd of young Chinese who helped me read characters that were written too cursively for me to make out. Of course all of the posters, some of them in rhyming style, attacked government corruption and called for freedom and democracy. Thousands of people going about their daily business would pause at the intersection to read them.

Just before I reached Tiananmen Square proper, there was a large open space where groups of people were camped. One of Beijing's double-length buses was parked there. Flags flew from its roof and a

"University students salute the people of Beijing!"

large white banner was draped over the side reading "UNIVERSITY
STUDENTS SALUTE THE PEOPLE OF BEIJING!"

Half a million people were in the square. I got past the outer
perimeter of young guards by showing them my Peking University
badge. It was extremely hot, and I bought a popsicle from a vendor
who was doing a brisk business. Something seemed to be going on
over at the square's east side, with a lot of people yelling and cheering.
I headed over to find it was a support demonstration made up primarily
of media workers. Groups marched by, shouting slogans like, "Down
with martial law!" and raising the V for victory sign. Their banners
were a catalog of China's mass media: New China News Agency,
People's Daily reporters, *Science and Technology Daily*, *China Youth
Magazine* editorial office, *Chinese Culture Daily*. Even more remarkable
was the presence of the Chinese Communist Central Party School—
future Communist leaders who carried a large banner that read,
"Oppose dictatorship. Oppose tyranny. Beijing belongs to the people
of Beijing."

After watching the demonstration a while, I rode to the Beijing
Hotel to buy film, and powdered milk for my morning coffee. Thus
fortified, I began the hot, dry, dusty ride back to the Shaoyuan

People's Daily *reporters. May 19.*

compound. The round trip took three hours—obviously, I wouldn't need to jog in Beijing this summer.

Back in my room, I switched on the air conditioner, took half a watermelon from the fridge, and prepared to bathe, when someone knocked on the door.

"Who is it?"

"*Shi women, it's us!*" I opened the door and was surprised to see two Peking University professors who had biked over to see me. I offered them a seat in the living room and poured a couple of glasses of ice water, but one glance at the watermelon on my desk and they grew embarrassed.

"You haven't eaten. You have to bathe first. We'll come back another time."

"No, no, no, *buyao keqi*, don't be so polite. It's all right. We can talk now."

And so we did, for half an hour. Their spirits were low. They had dreamed, maybe this time China would change. They said martial law certainly would be carried out eventually, and then the universities would be taken over by the army. "Once they've proclaimed it, they'll have to enforce it," one said.

Both had been through all this before. During the Cultural

Chinese Communists Central Party School. May 19.

Revolution, all the Peking University professors had been sent out to the countryside to work as peasants. This time they and 50 other professors had signed a big-character poster supporting the students and calling for the resignation of the vice minister of the State Education Commission, He Dongchang.

Concerning my research proposal, they agreed that not many writers would feel like discussing literature at this time, but they promised to help me collect interesting material on the "cultural exploration school" of writers. One of them gave me his new address before he left and said I must come to his house for dinner in a week or so, "after things settle down a bit."

I dined on peanuts, beer and watermelon while watching the CCTV news. Both the Beijing city and national news repeated the three martial law orders: all public assemblies are illegal; foreigners are to stay away from all illegal popular meetings; foreign reporters are forbidden to interview anyone, take pictures, or be present at illegal assemblies or activities.

I went to the Free Speech Triangle that night and taped student broadcasts from 8 to 10 P.M. Several thousand people were in front of the Student Broadcast Station and the nearby mess hall, male students sitting and standing around smoking cheap cigarettes, well-dressed

13

*Medical College contingent on May 19. The top banner
reads "Guan-dao is a Cancer of Corruption!" The sign they
are holding says, "Fellow students, here we come!"*

coeds walking up and down the pathway in front of the post office,
couples strolling hand-in-hand, families with small children, and a few
older faculty members. Merchants sold orange pop and popsicles from
two-wheeled carts, and they too had brought the whole family with
them. The vendors engaged in lively discussions with their customers.

People listened attentively to the loudspeakers. There were
numerous eyewitness stories of Beijing people, "little people," heroi-
cally stopping troop trucks as they attempted to roll into the city. Many
of the troops, the reports said, had not been informed of their mission.
When they saw the situations, many officers and men refused to go
forward.

All sorts of speculative political reports were broadcast: Zhao was
removed from office. Premier Li and President Yang have made a
successful *coup d'etat*. Actually, nobody was sure exactly to what degree
Deng was still in charge.

More letters of support were read, to the cheers of the crowd.
About 200,000 students and faculty were said to be occupying
Tiananmen Square at that time. The government had tried to cut off

food and water, but Beijing's university students and ordinary citizens were carrying supplies to them.

Deciding to try and contact the student leaders, at about 9:30 I walked to the dormitory that housed the Broadcast Station, which was close to the post office and the general store. I identified myself to the guard at the door and showed him my Beida (the shorthand word for Peking University) badge.

He wasn't very impressed. "What do you want to talk to the leaders about?" he asked in a suspicious voice.

"The Canadian Broadcasting Corporation is going to phone me from Vancouver one of these nights and I'd like to know what you want me to tell the people of Canada about your movement."

His eyes lit up. "Oh! Follow me."

We went up a narrow, unlighted staircase to the Student Broadcast Station, which consisted of two small, dimly lit rooms on the dorm's second floor. A table was set up in the doorway where a student waited to check the identification passes of anyone who wanted to enter.

"Wait here," he said, going in to explain what I was doing there.

Inside the inner room I could see two bunk beds and a table with several stereo cassette players of the type American teenagers carry around at the beach, as well as electronic equipment, a microphone, and a pile of papers with information to broadcast.

Finally a student with some authority in the movement—let's call him Zhang—came out and talked with me for a few minutes. He asked me to tell the Canadian people to "please support our struggle for the most elementary forms of human rights, that is freedom of speech, freedom of press, and freedom of assembly."

The most disheartening thing I heard at the Free Speech Triangle was that students expected the army to invade their campus and other universities tonight. And, *gansidui*, or "Dare to Die Brigades," would be patrolling Tiananmen Square all night looking for the army.

The Peking University Students Autonomous Association announced its intention to protect the campus and the broadcasting station. They would resist the army and the military rule of universities no matter what might happen. "They don't have anything," I thought, "and the government is so rotten." The situation was extremely tense throughout the night.

The army did not come last night as expected. A glance out of my fifth floor window on the morning of Sunday, May 21, convinced me that everything was normal. Shaoyuan workers were making hot water as usual. They had a black and white banner set up on the roof proclaiming support for the students, and they kept looking out over the back wall as if expecting troops to arrive at any minute.

No real news was reported on Beijing Central Radio. The Voice of America continued to be a major source of information about what was happening nine miles away in downtown Beijing.

I biked to the Free Speech Triangle and taped student broadcasts from 10 A.M. to 12:30 P.M., a fascinating miscellany of the genuine, the plausible, and the implausible:

—Martial law had not been carried out after 26 hours. That means, according to international law, that the government has no right to govern.

—The mayor of Shanghai has joined the pro-democracy demonstrations.

—Liang Xiang, the provincial governor of Hainan Island, has proclaimed his disassociation from the government. (Hearty applause.)

—An eyewitness said a *Lao da-ye* (polite Beijing dialect for old man) out for his constitutional in the early morning spotted some army troops near Capital Airport Road moving south toward the city. The old man immediately mobilized everyone in the neighborhood by beating on a pot. Old folk, mostly in their 60s and 70s, poured from their houses, surrounded the troops and prevented them from moving forward. The soldiers eventually marched back toward the airport. When the people returned in triumph to their homes, they laughed out loud to find their breakfast rice had burned.

—In another part of the city a group of elderly women with bound feet had formed themselves into the *Xiaojiaodui*, "Small Foot Brigade." They vowed to come out in force to stop the troops.

— *Lao niangmer*, "Little Old Ladies." (another Beijing term of endearment) were opening their homes all over the city to the students' Public Order Brigades.

Over the loudspeakers, a deep male voice intoned this poem, dedicated to the People's Liberation Army:

> Ask yourselves: who was it sent you into the army?
> It was the people,
> The far too-long suffering people of China's far too-
>   long suffering land.
> I would not oppose your firing on the people
> If they had committed some truly unpardonable
>   crime;
> Otherwise your gun barrels will weep,

Your bullets too, your bullets will cry.
When you train your eyes through the gun sights
Look over as well at the people's eyes;
Then resolve anew whom you should,
Should really be aiming at.

Approximately 1 million people were gathered on Tianan-men Square when I first arrived.

CHAPTER 2

SEARCHING FOR DEMOCRACY

U P UNTIL 1978, CHINA'S SEARCH FOR DEMOCRACY WAS dominated by three ideas: that democracy, or energy generated by popular political participation, is the secret of the strength of the European and American nations and their ability to dominate the world; that there is a natural harmony between the interests of the Chinese state and the Chinese people as a whole; that the nation, the state, and the government are identical. With the establishment of the Nationalist (KMT) and the Communist (CCP) parties on Leninist lines in the 1920s and 1930s, this third idea was extended to include the identity of the government with the party. China's rulers have regarded democracy merely as the most important means to "wealth and power" for the Chinese nation-state.

The idea of democracy as a means to wealth and power has served as justification for every democratic reform movement in China from the Hundred Days Reform of 1898 to the Deng Xiaoping reforms of the 1980s. The supposed identity of interests between the people and the government has hindered the emergence of an ideal of inalienable individual rights, as well as the establishment of political institutions to protect those rights. When the Communist Party took over in 1949, its leaders combined the traditional Confucian idea of a harmony of interests between the rulers and the ruled with the Leninist notion of a vanguard party that rules in the interests of the proletariat, or, in Maoist terms "the people." The so-called "dictatorship of the proletariat" or "People's Democratic Dictatorship," one of Deng Xiaoping's Four Cardinal Principles, has in practice simply been the dictatorship of the Communist Party and its paramount leader.

In more general terms, two complementary themes have dominated modern Chinese history: the search for wealth and power—to transform China's economic system, creating a strong and stable nation-state that could become one of the modern world's great powers;

and the struggle for freedom and democracy – to transform China's political system from an authoritarian to a more democratic one which guarantees popular sovereignty and human rights. Due to particular historical conditions from the 1890s to the 1970s, the search for wealth and power has always taken precedence over the extension of freedom and democracy.

In the 40 years of the People's Republic of China, ever greater numbers of intellectuals have come to believe that more personal political freedom and democracy are necessary to make China a rich and powerful nation. The harsh repression and wasteful policies of the Hundred Flowers and Anti-Rightist Campaigns of 1956–57, the Great Leap Forward of 1958–59, and the Cultural Revolution of 1966–76 caused them to believe that the primary threat to the nation now comes from the continuation of China's authoritarian political system. Such a system, they believe, is incapable of either economic or political modernization, unsuited for the production of wealth and power or the creation of freedom and democracy.

Deng Xiaoping, one of the original Communist revolutionaries, was savaged during the dementia of the Cultural Revolution. With the backing of Mao, Deng was stripped of power and sent to prison for several years. In 1972, he was freed, only to be attacked by Jiang Qing, Mao's wife, and the radical "Gang of Four."

After Mao died in 1976 and the country began to return to order, Deng managed to work his way back into the highest ranks of the Politburo. In 1978, he spearheaded a slow move toward economic reform. He also assigned Hu Yaobang to rehabilitate thousands of victims of the Cultural Revolution.

Meanwhile, interspersed with periods of violent repression, the ideal of democracy kept inching forward. From October 1978 to March 1979, a "Democracy Wall" was allowed to operate, upon which posters were erected freely criticizing government wrongdoing. The wall was extremely helpful for then-Vice Premier Deng and his "democratic" reformers as they sought power.

But once Deng and his cronies were firmly in control, the reformers were expendable. They were suppressed on Deng's orders.

After China's costly border war with Vietnam, Deng attacked the activists. On March 16 and 30, 1979, he laid out the Four Cardinal Principles as his response to their call for democracy. They are: China's economy must adhere to the socialist road; the people's democratic dictatorship is China's form of government; the Communist Party's leadership is unchallengeable; and Marxism-Leninism-Mao Zedong Thought is the official ideology.

Wei Jingsheng, an electrician who had been a Red Guard during the Cultural Revolution chaos and a soldier in the People's Liberation Army, called for a "fifth modernization," democracy. It would supplement the "Four Modernizations"—of industry, agriculture, science and technology—that guide state policy. In Democracy Wall posters he wrote, "Democracy is not a mere consequence, a certain stage in the development of society. It is the condition on which the survival of productive forces depends."

He maintained that democracy was the Chinese people's right. "When they ask for democracy, they are only demanding what is rightfully theirs," he declared.

Wei's ideas were considered a great threat to the hierarchy. He was tried, convicted and sentenced to fifteen years in prison for "counter-revolutionary crimes." He remains there today, if he has not died in prison from lack of medical attention, as Amnesty International fears he might have.

Yet in the seven years after the fall of the Democracy Wall Movement, China experienced periods of openness and liberalization. Among the factors that helped bring this about were the Communist Party's own repeated calls for more democratization and the policy of study abroad in which thousands of Chinese went overseas, particularly to the United States. Meanwhile, thousands of foreign scholars, business people, students and tourists visited China. Private companies, like the Stone Computer Corporation, were founded within China.

Intellectuals and the urban population in general gained a great deal of knowledge about freedom and the wealth of the industrialized democracies. Even in other communist countries, reform movements were gaining ground. Mikhail Gorbachev was loosening the bonds in the Soviet Union and its satellites, and change was sweeping his country, Poland and Hungary.

By the fall of 1986, Chinese students and intellectuals were calling for further political reforms to facilitate economic reform and make daily life more livable. Two of the most important reformers were Liu Binyan and Fang Lizhi.

My wife and I were living in China at the time, and we first met Liu during the Chinese Writers Association's first International Conference on Contemporary Chinese Literature. Held in Jinshan, a suburb of Shanghai, in November 1986, the conference was a model of the new openness. Liu, the vice chairman of the Chinese Writers

Association and one of the country's most famous writers, gave an electrifying lecture.

His 1979 novella, *People or Monsters?* had exposed the influence-peddling, bribery, corruption and embezzlement of a party clique in Heilongjiang Province. He demonstrated that the local Communist Party there was run on mafialike principles. "The Communist Party regulates everything, but it does not regulate the Communist Party," he wrote. Now he continued to speak out in a series of scathing indictments of party corruption and malfeasance, reports that made him the most respected and popular writer in China.

At the conference, Liu criticized the corruption of the present-day party, attacking party interference with literature and art. He spoke in a thorough, open, straightforward manner—as if he were a citizen of a democracy where this kind of criticism was an everyday occurrence protected by law. Nobody else at the conference spoke so fearlessly and with such confidence in the justice of his cause.

He charged that writers who were satisfied with the degree of literary freedom allowed at that time were "living in a dream," believing that they no longer had a responsibility to criticize social problems. He repeated a warning he had made during the reform movement of 1979, "People be on guard! It is still too early to be celebrating victory." Liu then reeled off a series of stories about contemporary corruption and injustice.

We wanted to talk with Liu Binyan privately, and to our delight, he invited us to travel with him to Tongji University, where he was giving a speech. It was one of a series of talks he was making all over China that summer and fall. The conference was anticlimactic after his speech, so we skipped its third day and accompanied him.

In the course of the most hair-raising taxi ride I've ever had, while the beat-up old cab was hurtling over huge potholes and weaving in and out among slow ox carts and on-coming trucks and buses, we discussed his travels to campuses. The students were in a discontented mood, he said. Liu was still optimistic about China's reforms, though he said he was only a token critic tolerated by the highest leadership. In fact, many of the leaders were opposed to letting him run loose, he added.

Suddenly the young driver got into the conversation: China should become part of the United States for 50 years, and then there might be real hope for the country, he said. Liu didn't agree with the young man's remark, but they indicated the mood of much of China's youth back then.

At Tongji University, Liu was greeted like a visiting celebrity, attracting a spontaneous audience that could not be reached by anybody in the top ranks of the leadership. In North America, only a rock star draws this kind of crowd. The auditorium where he spoke was filled to its capacity, more than 3,000. Liu talked for an hour on topics ranging from his experiences during the Anti-Rightist Campaign and the Cultural Revolution, to his investigations into corruption and injustice within the party. Pulling no punches, he told of persecution, false imprisonment, even execution—all of it carried out by local officials in every region of China *after* Deng came to power in 1978.

Liu continued his criticism during an hour-long question and answer period, but refused to answer some questions that were too dangerous. He would not directly answer whether China should have another political party, but replied in a way that indicated his feelings: "Nowhere is it written in Marx that there cannot be more than one political party under a socialist system."

Two students sitting directly behind us whispered, "That's not enough," and, "We've heard all this before."

When we returned to the literary conference we overheard a couple of bureaucrats commenting, "Binyan has been out stirring up the students again."

Another reformer traveling the university lecture circuit was Fang Lizhi, a famous astrophysicist and a reinstated party member who had also suffered during the Anti-Rightist Campaign and the Cultural Revolution. Recently appointed vice president of the University of Science and Technology in Hefei, he worked to protect student and faculty rights.

As early as 1980 Fang declared publicly that socialism was a dead ideology for China. In 1986 he emerged as a daring critic of party policy toward intellectuals. He advocated academic freedom, openness to new ideas from abroad, and intellectual resistance to party control.

Less than two weeks after Liu spoke at Tongji University, Fang addressed a similar crowd of students there. His defense of democracy represented the greatest breakthrough of the 1986–87 Democracy Movement. He stressed that human rights are the "critical component" of any democratic agenda. They should be the touchstone of democratization and should not be dependent on state or government largesse.

Fang emphasized the importance of the individual as opposed to the state or government, breaking with the ancient Chinese tradition of regarding the group as having greater value. Democracy flows from

23

the individual and the government has responsibilities toward him, he said.

He belittled the party's assertion that Chinese civilization is spiritually superior and is behind the west only in certain areas of technology. "Chinese intellectual life, material civilization, moral fiber, and government are in dire straits," he said. "The truth is, every aspect of the Chinese world needs to be modernized. . . . I think all-around openness is the only way to modernize. I believe in such a thorough and comprehensive liberalization because Chinese culture is not just backward in a particular respect, but primitive in an overall sense."

Liu and Fang were an inspiration to pro-democracy students, although certainly not the only reason for their campaigns. Starting in Shanghai on December 18 and continuing into the first week in January 1987, demonstrations spread to more than 100 campuses. This was the first great outpouring of public sentiment since the Cultural Revolution.

Calling for greater freedom, faster economic reforms, control of inflation, more democracy and human rights, and an end to corruption, the students now were speaking in western terms. In the past, their protests were couched in Marxist jargon.

"I have a dream, a dream of freedom," went one big-character poster, echoing Martin Luther King. "I have a dream of democracy. I have a dream of life endowed with human rights."

The demonstrations caught up with us that year in Hangzhou and Shanghai. Our bus from the Hangzhou railroad station was delayed by a student protest march. The American students on the bus were delighted to see their Chinese counterparts marching. They immediately opened the windows and started shouting questions and encouragements.

The two Peking University chaperones looked panicked and angry as the Chinese students shouted back. One of these officials in his early 50s reached over my shoulder and that of the student next to me, and slammed the window shut. "Mr. Duke, you must not let your students talk to the Chinese students! What they are doing is none of your business. You must tell your students not to interfere!"

Fortunately, he couldn't speak English, so he didn't understand what I was telling my students: "Hold it down until we get to the College of Fine Arts dormitory. Then you're on your own. Understand?" Later, several stayed up all night in the bitter cold fraternizing with the noisy demonstrators.

Under Party General Secretary Hu Yaobang and Premier Zhao

Ziyang, the government reacted with great restraint. Students arrested in Tiananmen Square demonstrations were quickly released, and steps were taken to improve living conditions at the universities.

The conservatives counterattacked in the second week of January 1987, a thrust mounted with Deng's full concurrence. Deng made Hu a scapegoat in order to appease ideological hard-liners. Hu was suddenly fired as General Secretary for being too soft on "bourgeois liberalization" and the student demonstrations, among other things.

Fang Lizhi, Liu Binyan and the writer Wang Ruowang were publicly expelled from the Communist Party. Then the media whipped up an intense campaign against "bourgeois liberalization" and "ultra-democracy." The papers were full of long articles about social problems like racism, drug addiction, and crime in the United States, much of it true but all of it irrelevant to the questions of democracy and human rights in China.

Zhao was promoted to General Secretary and managed to confine the anti-bourgeois liberalization campaign mostly within the party. The backlash didn't last long. Unlike previous campaigns within the party against "rightist elements," virtually no one cooperated with the leaders.

An ironic twist was that Fang's and Liu's speeches were required reading for all party members, who were supposed to hold study sessions and criticize their ideas. The result was that many more people came to agree with them. A well-known literary figure told me that a 60-year-old party cadre from Hunan called him to say, "That kid Fang Lizhi tells it the way it is."

One member described a criticism meeting as, "The leadership reads their accusations, we all sit there silently, the meeting's adjourned, and we go home."

Another said, "The leadership invited me to dinner. They wanted to take my picture and say in the press I was there supporting their criticism of Liu Binyan. I told them I was sick. End of discussion."

The campaign petered out toward the end of summer. The situation soon improved to the extent that dissidents could once again talk to foreigners.

Following the usual custom of Chinese intellectuals in times of party persecution, every couple of weeks that spring we sent Liu Binyan a get-well card. We wrote "We hope your health improves. Take care of yourself." Health is a code word for the political situation. He didn't answer our first few cards, but in late June he finally wrote to us saying he would like to meet with us, but not in a private home and not

I visited Liu Binyan on July 8, 1987, thirty years after he was first branded a Rightist.

alone. He gave us a list of reliable friends to contact to set up a meeting with him in a public place. We chose a writer we knew and he went with us.

On July 8, 1987, we met Liu Binyan in a restaurant in Beijing, where he was having lunch with a group of editors and reporters. Liu commented it was exactly 30 years to the day since he had been branded a "rightist" in 1957. It was a day to celebrate, and we did.

First we went to the Central Art Academy to view a one-man show that was being kept open an additional day especially for him and another special guest. The artist, Zeng Xiaofeng, was a very talented young man from Yunnan whose works combined folk motifs with modern Western techniques reminiscent of Salvador Dali. The other special guest turned out to be Bette Bao Lord. As the wife of the American Ambassador, Winston Lord, she helped many Chinese writers and artists with their careers. She and Liu had a long tte-a-tte in the corner while we talked with several other guests who arrived with her. Next we stopped at a coffee shop and talked for a couple of hours, then ended up at a hotel restaurant where we spent several more hours eating and talking.

Liu Binyan smoked cigarettes one after another, the only thing he has in common with Deng Xiaoping, as he offered his views on China's political and economic situation. We told him what other mutual friends said about the improving situation, but he was far less optimistic. He said that Deng Xiaoping would not allow anyone to slow down economic reform, but he was certain that the campaign to criticize him and Fang Lizhi came directly from Deng himself.

Deng Xiaoping, Liu affirmed, is basically opposed to democracy and the rule of law. There was a jingle going around in Beijing that went, "Freedom can't be obtained, Democracy can't be proclaimed, The government can't be run down, Xiaoping can't step down."

Asked what they would do if they were suddenly in charge, Liu and the writer friend of his gave the same answer many others had: free the press. The government should allow the newspapers, radio and television to report on the real problems facing the country and not just offer soporific fairy-tale success stories.

There was one thing, Liu said, we should let the outside world know. There are many people in the Communist Party whose hands are still bloody from what they did in the Cultural Revolution, but they continue to enjoy rank and privilege. They continue to perpetrate heinous acts of injustice. He related a gruesome example. In Gan County in Jiangxi Province a young woman worker was sent to prison in the late sixties after her boyfriend denounced her for criticizing the Gang of Four. She was not executed until *after* the Gang of Four was arrested in October 1976. After she was killed, her corpse was both raped and mutilated. Her executioners actually cut off her breasts.

Our writer friend then told us another equally horrible Cultural Revolution story. An eyewitness told him that whenever people are taken to the execution ground, an ambulance goes along with them. He thought that was very humane, taking care of the victim right up to the time of speedy execution.

"Oh no!" said his informant. "That's not it at all. The ambulance is there to retrieve the vital organs immediately after death in order to take them to the hospital where aging high-ranking officials are waiting for transplants."

"One time," he went on, "they were in such a hurry to save some old cadre's life that they removed a woman's kidneys before they shot her. They did it without anesthetics. Just cut her open, took out her kidneys, stuffed some cotton in her side, dragged her out screaming in pain, and shot her."

Many such killings took place in the early days after the fall of the Gang of Four when their former followers tried to kill as many of their possible accusers as they could.

When we returned to Peking University that night and told an older professor how shocked we were at these stories, he said, "Right, things like that happened all the time. In a village just outside of Beijing, near the end of the Cultural Revolution, the local party authorities tied up the entire population of over 100 people with high tension electrical wiring. Then they turned on the electricity and killed them all. Nobody knows what their crime was supposed to be."

In 1989, the Democracy Movement resurfaced with greater force than ever. An intense power struggle was unfolding at the highest reaches of the party while an equally intense intellectual ferment was developing in China's urban universities, literary groups and research institutes.

The inner party struggle was primarily concerned with power, with who was to have what power, and how that power to determine the nation's future was to be passed on to their successors. The intellectual ferment was primarily concerned with solving the related problems of official corruption, nepotism, inflation, and economic dislocation that had resulted from the party's mismanagement of the economic reform. It was also concerned with increasing the scope of political freedom and popular participation in the decision-making processes that determine the goals and the pace of political and economic reform.

The settlement of the power struggle led to the Tiananmen Massacre, the dismissal of Zhao Ziyang as General Secretary, the re-emergence of a group of retired octogenarians as the real governing power, and a nationwide purge of dissident intellectuals. The intellectual ferment on college campuses and academic salons grew into the largest spontaneous popular movement for freedom ever mounted against any Communist government in power.

On January 16, Fang wrote a private letter to Deng, addressing him in his capacity as chairman of the Central Military Commission. He called on him to declare a general amnesty for "political prisoners" in honor of the coming of several important anniversaries, including the fortieth anniversary of the founding of the People's Republic in 1949.

On February 13, the poet Bei Dao and 32 other prominent intellectual and literary figures signed an open letter to the Standing

Committee of the National People's Congress and the Communist Party Central in support of Fang's letter. Just under two weeks later, 42 Beijing scientists and intellectuals signed another open letter, this one addressed to General Secretary Zhao and nearly every important committee in the government.

The scientists' letter, unprecedented in the history of the People's Republic, called for further democratic reforms—including freedom of speech, publication, and press—as absolutely essential to the success of China's continued economic improvements and the advance of science. They called for the release from prison or labor camps of all young people convicted of "crimes of thought."

Fang published an article in the Hong Kong journal *The Nineties*, which appeared simultaneously in translation in the February 2 edition of the *New York Review of Books*. He called for the formation of "pressure groups" from China's new "middle class" to push for major reforms in many areas, including guarantees of human rights, establishment of a free economic system, renunciation of force concerning Taiwan, applying the rule of law to the party and its leaders, and a revision of the Constitution to eliminate vague political terms like "class struggle" and "counter-revolution."

Fang made international headlines on February 26 when he and his wife, Li Shuxian, were prevented by the Public Security Bureau from attending a farewell banquet given by President Bush at the conclusion of his visit to China. Fang then told a press conference at the Shangri-la Hotel that he and other dissidents were calling for extremely basic things—freedom of speech, press, assembly and travel.

By then, many other Chinese regarded democracy and human rights in the same way, as a legacy rightfully theirs.

On March 14, another public letter came out in support of Fang's call for amnesty. This one, signed by 43 literary figures and addressed to the National People's Congress, was organized by Dai Qing, the reporter from the *Guangming Daily* who later tried to negotiate with the students. It was signed by professor Yan Jiaqi, elected on September 24 as chairman of the Paris-based Federation for a Democratic China.

On April 15, in the midst of this public drive for democracy, the deposed but highly- regarded Hu Yaobang died. The students of Peking University and Beijing Normal University seized this opportunity to make a symbolic protest against political corruption and the suppression of free expression.

The first march from the university area to Tiananmen Square attracted about 20,000 students and other young people. They asked for a posthumous re-evaluation of the case against Hu.

The official response was the devastating April 26 editorial in the *People's Daily* branding the movement a well-organized "disturbance" harboring ulterior motives opposed to the interests of the Party and the nation.* University loudspeakers broadcast intimidating warnings to the students not to leave their campuses. Security forces visited foreign scholars on university campuses warning them not to join in student demonstrations.

The next day the students replied with an angry demonstration, 150,000 strong, that peacefully broke through police lines to the cheers of thousands of onlookers and reached Tiananmen Square. It was a daring act of political defiance of government orders to seal off the square. The students demanded a dialogue with the government.

Officials promised they would give them an answer by May 11, but the date came and went: Zhao Ziyang wanted the dialogue but he couldn't get the hard-liners to go along.

On May 13, two days before Gorbachev's historic visit to Beijing, 1,000 students began a hunger strike in Tiananmen Square. The number soon grew to 3,000, and they gained the support of nearly every part of Beijing society. On the day of the Soviet leader's visit, 300,000 students and workers backing the hunger strikers swarmed into Tiananmen Square and prevented Gorbachev's scheduled stop at this central shrine to the revolution. They began the occupation of Tiananmen.

Zhao convened a meeting of the Politburo Standing Committee on May 16 and called for the repudiation of the *People's Daily* editorial. The Politburo refused.

In a meeting with Gorbachev later that day, Zhao publicly revealed that the Thirteenth Party Congress had passed a secret resolution in 1987 retaining Deng Xiaoping as the final arbiter of every major policy decision. It was immediately obvious to everybody that Zhao was telling the Chinese protesters as well as the world audience that Deng and not himself was responsible for the leadership's position toward the Democracy Movement.

It was a serious mistake. For the first time in the history of the

---

*   See note on page 31.

Chinese Communist Party, a general secretary publicly criticized the unofficial paramount leader. He committed the unpardonable sin of publicly displaying a split in the highest leadership.

Several of Zhao's intellectual supporters, including professor Yan Jiaqi, issued a declaration May 17 criticizing Deng in the most uncompromising terms. "The Qing Dynasty has been dead for 76 years," they wrote, "but China still has an uncrowned emperor on the throne, an aged and muddle-headed despot."

For Deng, that was the last straw; Zhao had to go.

In the early hours that day, Zhao released a written statement saying the students' enthusiasm for democracy, reform, and an end to corruption, were extremely valuable. The party leaders took everyone's "reasonable opinions" very seriously, and the government absolutely would not take reprisals against the students, he said.

But by then, he was isolated in the Politburo.

His statement was too late to prevent the largest protest demonstrations in the history of the People's Republic. The students were joined by everyone from intellectuals and journalists to street vendors, factory workers, teachers, Foreign Ministry staffers, bus drivers, police and party officials.

On May 17 and 18, more than one million people marched to the square from every part of Beijing. Some eyewitnesses told me it was more like 2 to 2.5 million. Demonstrations spread to most of China's major cities. Clearly, the government had lost control.

NOTE

The April 26 editorial reflected the views of Deng Xiaoping himself which never really changed from then until the June 4 massacre. A summary of his views at that time follows: "the student movement is an anti-Party, anti-socialist disturbance; Hu Yaobang [meaning Zhao Ziyang] was soft on 'bourgeois liberalization;' the peasants are not a problem; the workers are basically stable, though there are some unstable elements; we must rightly employ the People's Democratic Dictatorship; we can have a dialogue with the students, but we cannot allow improper behavior; we should avoid shedding blood as far as possible, but we cannot completely avoid it; we need a strong editorial to carry out a nationwide political struggle; they are using the freedom and democracy in the Constitution to struggle against us, but Beijing has the ten anti-demonstration regulations to use against them; if China allowed demonstrations, there would be no stability, as I told President Bush; if they establish autonomous student associations, abolish them; that's a Cultural Revolution trick in order to create chaos; there are only 60,000 students boycotting classes and we must protect the 100,000 who are still attending classes; the workers, peasants, and Party cadres support us; we also have several million Liberation Army soldiers, so what is there to fear; we must put this new-style student movement down quickly; it won't do to give in as the Polish Communist Party has; the People's Democratic Dictatorship comes in very handy now; if we didn't have the Four Cardinal Principles, they would be uncontrollable."

CHAPTER 3

VOICES OF THE PEOPLE

THAT WAS THE SITUATION WHILE I WAS MAKING MY WAY to Beijing in May 1989, flying in from Hong Kong after a conference in Taiwan. Entitled "Social and Political Changes in Mainland China: the Literary View," the conference reviewed the gains and losses for Chinese literature and culture during the past ten years.

The most interesting part of the conference was a private briefing by professor King-yuh Chang, director of the Institute of International Relations. In a very frank 40-minute talk, he outlined Taiwan's hopes for a stable future and good relations with all of the Pacific Rim nations. He said that Taiwan's multi-party politics would continue to flourish, that within four years all of the aging members of the National Congress would be retired and replaced by people elected in Taiwan, and that the advocacy of only two things — communism and Taiwan independence — were expressly forbidden by the constitution of the Republic of China, a term he never used. He fielded well many blunt questions about the Taiwan Independence Movement, the People's Progressive Party, and relations with the mainland. We all left the meeting quite impressed. One of the Australians even remarked on the "strange outbreak of reason" in Taibei.

The Democracy Movement in Beijing was on everyone's mind those first days of May. Australian scholars said their Chinese students had been telling them something big and ominous was about to happen in China, maybe an explosion on a par with the Boxer Rebellion. I spent every morning in my hotel room reading all of the mainland news in Taiwan's leading dailies — the demonstrations in Tiananmen Square on May 4, the start of the hunger strike coinciding with Gorbachev's visit, the support marches by intellectuals, writers and reporters. I knew many of the people in the news stories both as personal friends and as research subjects.

I was amazed to read a fierce article about the Chinese Communist

Party, written for a Taiwan newspaper by Liu Binyan. Liu, who had become a research fellow at Harvard University, tore into the party's corruption and venality in a manner reminiscent of articles in the Nationalists' papers of the 1960s.

I reached Hong Kong on May 14. The atmosphere there was even more electrified by the news from Beijing, because the British have agreed to pull out of the crown colony in 1997 and turn control over to China. On May 17, I stayed glued to the TV in my room at the Kowloon YMCA watching more than a million people demonstrate for democracy in Beijing. It was hard to believe I was seeing the same place that was so quiet in 1987.

On the Cathay Pacific flight from Hong Kong to Beijing on May 18, I was seated in the same row with a couple of retired Nationalist soldiers. Originally from Shandong Province, they were making their first trip home from Taiwan after a separation of 40 years. It was an indication of the new openness and the better relations between the breakaway province and the mainland, that these old enemies could freely return.

When we reached Beijing, our landing was delayed for over an hour by a thunderstorm. As we circled in a holding pattern, I thought the storm a perfect symbol for the democratic movement raging in the country below.

Almost everyone I talked with or eavesdropped on in those first days back at Beijing—including staffers at the Shaoyuan Guest House complex, Peking University teachers and workers, taxi drivers, Peking Hotel staffers, people of all ages on the street—backed the demonstrators.

In fact, during the hour-long drive from the airport to the university, the cab driver said the entire city of Beijing supported the students. He and most of his fellow drivers had taken students to Tiananmen for free more times than he could remember. "This government is just too corrupt; they've got to do something about it," he said.

Hauling my two 70-pound suitcases up five flights of stairs to my room in the Shaoyuan Guest House, I was soon drenched with sweat. I turned on the air conditioning and flipped on the color television. Looking out at me were Jane Wyman and the others of "Falcon Crest," engaging in one of their interminable arguments over land and water rights in the Napa-Sonoma Valley wine country—and they were arguing in perfect Mandarin. Sexy, violent, money-grubbing "bourgeois liberalization" was alive and well on CCTV, I thought.

Staffers at the guest house all remembered me and were glad to tell about the Democracy Movement, which was all anyone wanted to talk about at that time. They all supported the students and had been to the square to prove it.

"Surely not *everybody* in this building," I said, remembering that party bureaucrats worked on the third floor.

"Yes, yes, even the *Liuban* (Office of Foreign Student Affairs) sent a delegation to support the students!"

Looking at their beaming faces and listening to them talk enthusiastically about the demonstrations, I remembered the way they moped slowly through their tasks in 1987. Back then, one of them had summed up their philosophy in one word, *couhe*, muddle through. "That's all we do, just muddle through."

Although they had reasonably good jobs for unskilled laborers, life offered few chances for enthusiasm in those days. Now they had hope, and something to cheer about.

One friend told me, "We've all been to the square to support the students." Even a conservative he mentioned had gone, a person whom I'd never imagine doing such a thing. People openly cursed the governmental corruption known as *guan-dao*, "official turnaround," in which officials take advantage of their status to buy industrial raw material at low prices and sell them to factories and other enterprises at a great mark-up. This sort of thing is rampant among the hated *gaogan zidi*, "golden children," the sons and daughters of high party cadres.

I had lunch with an American scholar who had been in Beijing since the previous summer. For weeks my friend had felt pessimistic about the students' chance to win changes. He had kept predicting a government crackdown every day, until the May 17 demonstrations of more than a million people. After that he didn't see how the government could suppress them. He said he could not imagine "how they could be that stupid." The government would have to do something to appease the people now, he believed.

What none of us realized then was that the die was cast. Party Secretary Zhao Ziyang had wept when he visited the students at Tiananmen May 19 because his fate and theirs were sealed. He had given his valediction.

When I visited the Free Speech Triangle after martial law took effect, the loudspeakers were used less for theoretical arguments and more for news and strategy. One morning, a tape of the Voice of America's Chinese language morning broadcast was played, with an analysis by a *Washington Post* reporter that a high-level power struggle was going on to determine Deng Xiaoping's successor. The army was reluctant to decide the issue, the reporter said.

Student announcers claimed that "the Old Emperor," as they referred to Deng, was in Hunan trying to find some People's Liberation Army generals to support his martial law policies. Nobody really knew where Deng was.

Meanwhile, troops continued to stop or turn back as soon as they read last week's newspapers, the students said. Some soldiers told the protesters that they were not allowed to watch any TV news for the past week, and were ordered to read the April 26 editorial in the *People's Daily*. Tears appeared in their eyes as they said, "We were tricked into coming here," according to the students.

Letters of support from all over the world and throughout China were being read over the loudspeakers. The most interesting was from a group of researchers who, the report claimed, made up part of Zhao's "brain trust." They called for an emergency meeting of the National People's Congress or the Party Central Committee to discuss the current situation and propose remedies.

More than 30 members of the Standing Committee of the National People's Congress, believed to be supporters of Zhao, wrote to Party Central calling for an emergency meeting. They seemed to be pushing for Zhao Ziyang to be "elected" as head of the government rather than placed in power by Deng Xiaoping. Of course, they said, they did not know if Zhao would accept.

As General Secretary of the Communist Party, Zhao should have been de facto head of the government anyhow. But actually he was in no position to help his brain trust or any other followers.

Former Ambassador Lord made a statement of support for the Democracy Movement, which was broadcast as recorded from the Voice of America. It was greeted with loud applause.

About 300,000 people were still occupying Tiananmen Square. Students said they expected at least a week-long struggle to end martial law. They thought the government would change its mind and meet at least some of their demands.

The protesters in the square were supplied with food and water by the people of Beijing and other students. Later it turned out that much of the great costs were met by private enterprises, such as the Stone Computer Company and the hundreds of *getihu*.

Some Beijing residents had started panic buying of foodstuffs. Students were asked to organize Propaganda Brigades (*quanshuodui*, literally "persuasion brigades") to prevent the development of such a risky situation. Panic buying would be dangerous to their cause, since if food supplies grew short it would bolster the government's contention that there was such a serious "disturbance" in Beijing that the army was needed. It would be an excuse for a military crackdown.

Letters were read from students both in China and abroad, asking that special party meetings be held to vote on the correct path of action.

A Peking University student made a long, impassioned speech calling on all those "theorists of democracy"—his fellow graduate students, professors and others—to leave their books and come out now to join them in direct action. He first upbraided any fellow classmates who still remained in their dormitories instead of marching to the front lines at Tiananmen.

"The entire nation is rising to the call today," he said. "What can we accomplish in our rooms? . . . Revolution means taking concrete action."

It was time for the "elite intellectuals" to step bravely forward and be tested, he said. "Let us not act like human beings at home only and like dogs in public . . . . The time for us to act like human beings has already begun."

The student described the surprised reaction of the troops when they were told that this was a patriotic movement for democracy, and not some anarchistic disturbance. Like thousands of others, he believed that the "people's army" would not fire on the people.

"Once they learned the true situation, they resolutely sided with us," he said. "Therefore, we should not regard our army as our enemy. They are and will always be our brothers, members of our family. So when we meet them, we should not say anything to hurt their feelings."

A poem on a dormitory wall, pasted over another big-character poster dated May 1, said:

> The premise of democracy is the awakening of the masses.
> Snail government and crocodile government rule generation after generation;
> They're used to deception, but history cannot be deceived.
> Government,
> You are brain dead,
> Even hot-blooded youth cannot awaken you.
> Only the corrupt need to control people;

Only fools want paternalistic officials.
Where the master is, there is democracy;
Nonsense, nonsense,
Isn't everybody sleeping quite soundly?!

More troops were reported to be arriving all the time to encircle Beijing, though they were being stopped by the crowds.

Every few minutes the Broadcast Station would issue an "emergency announcement" that volunteers should line up in front of Building 29, organize themselves into a Public Order Brigade, and leave for one of the areas where soldiers were on the move.

The most dangerous places were Nan Yuan Airport south of the city, where 7,000 to 10,000 soldiers were reported to have landed; the Marco Polo Bridge, where many trucks filled with troops had been sighted, units believed to be from Mongolia; and the road south of Liuliqiao, a bridge into Beijing from the southwest, where students and townspeople had halted 40 trucks and three tanks.

Near the Liuliqiao bridge, people slept on tank treads. A student who had just returned from spending the night there said the treads were *ting shufu*, "pretty comfortable," but added that the students were exhausted. More volunteers were needed all the time.

The troops at the airport were supposed to be from the back country of Guangxi Province, men who knew nothing about the past weeks' events in Beijing. Student strategists expected them to try and break out that night, because Vice Premier Wan Li was believed stuck there after his return from the United States. Wan had cut his visit short because of the trouble at home.

An eyewitness said riot police on the outskirts of Beijing beat up some students, including women. When peasants in a nearby field saw what was happening, they became enraged. They ran over and lit into the police with hoes, bloodying many heads and sending the police running. Loud applause from the crowd.

Another witness told me the peasants who participated in this and other battles were from the *Sijiqing* (Evergreen) Regional Government, a former model commune outside Beijing that I visited with my students in September 1986. The commune had prospered as a result of the economic reforms since 1979.

In the afternoon I went to Haidian Township to buy paper and cassette tapes. The streets were jammed with people. Shops were operating normally, and the *getihu* were busily hawking every kind of product. It was just like any other Sunday afternoon except that the

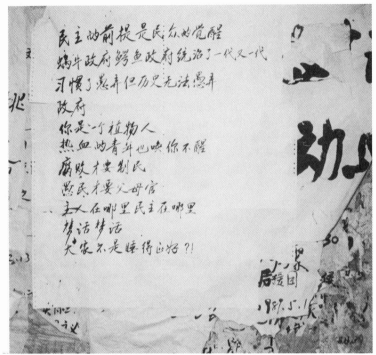

The premise of democracy is the awakening of the masses.

shop girls were actually friendly, laughing and joking with customers—most unusual for Beijing.

A small crowd gathered around me when I asked for a box of ten tapes at the state-run department store. Surprised that I wanted so many at one time, they asked me to read the English labels on the various varieties and tell which brand was best. When I asked, they all said they supported the students.

After dinner I returned to the Broadcast Station and had long discussions with some of the hundreds of people gathered there. They told me the government had discredited itself by calling out troops to "restore order" where there was no disorder.

The question on everybody's mind was whether the army would obey orders. Rumors spread that Beijing Regional Commander Zhou Yibing and Defense Minister Qin Jiwei were resisting martial law. The struggle for control of the People's Liberation Army was beginning.

Beijing University's emergency clinic continued to receive sick and exhausted students from Tiananmen. Families in the area were welcoming students into their homes, so they could rest and dine before they went out to rejoin the Public Order Brigades.

This must surely be the people of Beijing's finest hour. People were gathered in clumps all over Haidian and on the Peking University campus to express their disgust and hatred of the government. It was very moving to listen to the students' broadcasts and I grew choked up several times during their "critical reports," especially those coming from Chinese students in the United States. It brought back for me all of the idealism of the anti-Vietnam War demonstrations in Berkeley in the 1960s and early 1970s. These people's sentiments were so genuine but their government was so terrible, it made an outside observer feel sadly impotent and angry at the same time. But they were far too busy for all that.

After breakfast on Monday, May 22, I went to the campus post office to mail some letters and look at the literary journals. The magazine seller, a man in his 60s who had been helpful to me in finding works of certain writers when I was here before, still remembered me—"but your beard's a lot whiter now," he said.

He asked which writers I was interested in reading this time, and I gave him a list. On a shelf behind him were a large number of journals, some of them serious, but most of them with covers displaying pretty models and actresses from Taiwan, Hong Kong, or the United States.

None of the magazines seemed to be selling at that time. The students who came into the shop while I was there were looking for newspapers, especially the *Beijing Youth Daily* and the English language paper, *China Daily*. I said good-bye to the magazine man and went outside to mail my letters.

As I dropped the letters in the box, a lengthy big-character poster caught my eye. Entitled, "Public Notice," it was signed by the magazine seller.

> Ever since my fellow students [as he called them, they
> could have just as well been his children and he
> certainly regarded them as such] started fasting, I have
> been very troubled. I've been unable to eat or sleep for
> worrying about the students' health. In order that the
> students can drink a little more water, I personally
> volunteer to donate all my private proceeds from the
> next three days' sales to the fasting students, thus
> doing what little I can to show my support.

In signing the announcement, he was taking a personal risk, adding one more name to the lists of those who might find themselves

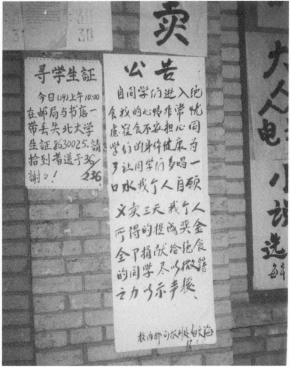

The magazine seller's big character poster.

"rectified" in the coming months if martial law were truly imposed. It was the type of support announcement I noticed all over Beijing.

The Student Broadcast Station was going strong as usual, making appeals one after another for students to go to Building 29, form into Public Order Brigades, and propagandize the soldiers.

In front of this building, young men and women were lining up in the middle of the courtyard between the dorms. They carried red or white banners with Peking University written on them in large yellow or black characters. A young man smiled broadly as he held up a banner and tried to get people to line up behind him. "Protect Zhongnanhai, protect Zhongnanhai!" he shouted.

Zhongnanhai is the compound where the Party Central officials live, close to Tiananmen. I laughed out loud and marveled at the students' sense of humor in the face of real danger.

Back at the Broadcast Station, I heard a report that soldiers and

"Baowei Zhongnanhai! Protect Zhonganhai!" A good-humored student prepares to join the May 22 Public Order Brigade.

citizens had clashed near Liuliqiao Bridge, where the people had stopped the convoy. Soldiers hit some people with sticks in order to force their way through them. The people were trying to prevent their moving forward, and the troops pulled back to a base area to wait, the eyewitness said.

Wait for what? I presumed it was to await the outcome of a struggle in the top leadership on whether to attack or move closer to Zhao's proposal to hold a dialogue with the students.

I biked to Tiananmen Square at about two o'clock. It was the same scene with hundreds of thousands of people, but this day the temperature was about 90 degrees. Many small piles of garbage were scattered around, and a strong smell of urine wafted over from the northwest end of the square, toward the Great Hall of the People.

If you have ever spent two days and three nights in a hard berth compartment of a Chinese train, as we did in 1986-87, or, worse yet, on the hard seats, as most Chinese do, you would not think the camp was particularly filthy.

Approaching the square near the Great Hall of the People, I saw a small crowd in the street and stopped to see what was going on. In

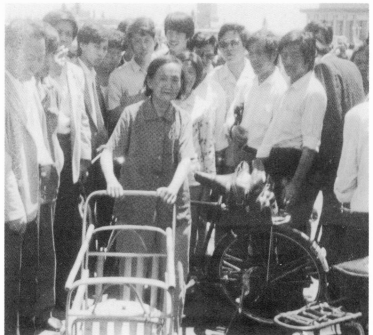

The old lady vigorously spouted Cultural Revolution slogans.

the center a woman about 70 years old was pushing a bamboo baby stroller with two large cooking pots on it. She wore a blue shirt and loose gray cotton pants; she had just delivered the two full pots of hot food to the square's occupiers and was taking the empties back for more.

This woman was one of the few "crazies" I've ever seen in China. In a high-pitched voice, she kept shouting four-character rhyming slogans from the Cultural Revolution. The crowd treated her with great politeness, but they were obviously delighted at the diversion.

I showed her my camera and she stopped spouting slogans just long enough for me to snap her picture. Then she pushed through the onlookers and wobbled away, swaying gently from right to left in time with her political rhymes of a bygone time.

On the other side of the square, across from the Revolutionary History Museum, people were bringing in cooked food. Taxis were filled with loaves of bread, boxes of dried noodles, stacks of disposable chopsticks. Cars and small white vans were carrying in water.

A woman brings steamed noodles for the students.

I stopped a woman as she pedaled by on a three-wheel pedicab with buckets of hot soup and a load of hot *mantou*, a kind of steamed bun the size of a muffin. "Can I take your picture?"

Embarrassed but smiling, she said, "I didn't come here to have my picture taken."

"Yes, of course, but I want to let the world know how the people of Beijing support the students."

"Well . . ."

I photographed her in front of a line of students who were waiting to pick up bowls of noodles from a temporary soup kitchen. She wheeled her load to another kitchen, where her friends were dishing noodles to the students. Some of the kids had their own bowls, but many were using the vendors' bowls after they were dipped in buckets of cold water to "wash" them.

The Chinese have a saying, *Bu gan bu jing, chi le mei bing,* "It's not at all clean, but you don't get sick from eating it." Nevertheless, the Chinese Red Cross issued warnings every day about the worsening sanitary and health conditions on the square.

On my way home I stopped now and then to read big-character posters. Draped over a public announcement at the entrance to the Palace Museum, formerly the Forbidden City, was this message: "In order to achieve victory (we shall) begin to eat tomorrow. Li Peng, do not cheat the people. By refusing to carry on a direct dialogue for over a month now, you have become the chief criminal oppressor of the students."

A 36-line pentasyllabic poem was pasted over an entire shop window, a scathing criticism of corruption as an integral part of the political system. It equated Deng with Chairman Mao as one who cheated the people in order to take power and then betrayed the people's trust by protecting corruption in high places.

> The system produces corruption
> The corrupt rely on the system.

It charged that for the officials to eat one meal, the common people labor an entire year; to fatten a few, they exhaust a billion people.
The last lines called for the citizens to

> Overthrow the old system
> Return power to the people
> Elect good people to office
> And impeach the rotten ones.

Receipt for a donation to Peking University students.

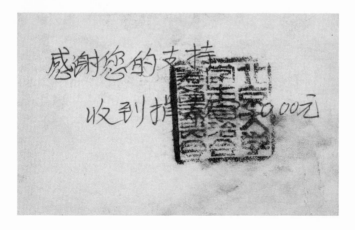

CHAPTER 4

MARCHING FOR CHINA

TUESDAY, MAY 23, WAS A GREAT DAY FOR CHINA AND I had a small part in it. At 9:30 A.M., I went to the Student Broadcast Station, arriving just in time to hear an interesting critical essay. It claimed that Mao did not build Marxist socialism in China but only continued the feudal traditions of the Chinese empire, with himself as an uncrowned emperor. Today's Communist Party and its leaders, said the writer, were no more than a new imperial bureaucracy every bit as corrupt as that of the late Qing Dynasty, which began in 1644 and was overthrown by the Revolution of 1911.

When the essay ended to scattered applause from the usual breakfasting audience, I went over to the student headquarters and found the leader I'd met earlier. I told him I intended to write a report about the Beida students' ideas and activities, and asked him to save all their written material for me. He said he would and introduced me to the people inside Building 29.

Brigade leaders were presenting their student identity cards to students seated in the doorway of a dormitory room, outlining their brigade's missions, and receiving the necessary propaganda materials. After an introduction, students in the headquarters gladly supplied me with copies of all the leaflets that had been printed so far. At that time, I suddenly realized I had not yet given any tangible support, and said I wanted to give them some money.

They looked at each other in embarrassment. Then I understood I had not used the right word. I corrected myself, saying I wanted to donate some money.

"Oh, you want to donate money," one replied. "We'll find the responsible person. Hey! The professor wants to donate some money! Where's the treasurer?"

I was led into an adjacent room, where a young man seated at a table accepted my donation and issued a receipt. Printed on the top were the words, "Peking University Students Autonomous Association Planning Committee," and below that, in larger characters, "Souvenir of Donation." On the reverse, the treasurer wrote, "Thank you for your support. Received donation of ___ yuan." Then he stamped it with the official red seal of the Beida Students Autonomous Association.

The living quarters were a mess, with papers and debris scattered all over. But their minds were clear and their dignity was intact; they weren't accepting charity but were happy to get contributions for the cause. And they gave lovely receipts.

I told them the outside world was well-informed about events in China, that the government's news blackout had failed so far. "Great," they said.

Shortly afterward, an "emergency announcement" came over the loudspeakers that a citywide demonstration would begin at 1:30 that afternoon. People were to form up at Jianguomen, "Establish the Nation Gate" in the east, and Fuxing Gate in the west, then converge on Tiananmen Square.

I left on my bike at eleven o'clock, but my derriere was so sore from two days of biking that I got only as far as the Xi Yuan Hotel. There I persuaded a pleasant taxi driver to put my bike in the trunk of his cab and drive me to the Jianguo Hotel, which is about five miles east of Tiananmen. The driver was around 40, articulate, and dressed in shorts. He was out of uniform—they're supposed to wear suits even in the summer heat. All the way down Sanlihe Road and east past the great square, he praised the students and cursed the government. He had an especially low opinion of Premier Li Peng. Commenting on Li's martial law address, he said, "Li Peng's speech didn't even sound like a premier. So incompetent, so inept, so bumbling and incapable. How can he be a premier?"

Responding to my question, he said the bosses of his taxi company had not expressed any opinions about the student demonstrations and martial law, but that they never bothered him and other drivers for driving students all around the city for free.

Na jiushi moren, "They're just silently admitting the students are right," he said. He let me off across from the Jianguo Hotel because, he said, he wasn't properly dressed to unload customers at a tourist hotel.

After a hamburger and a milkshake, I pedaled over to the Jianguo Gate assembly point and met up with several thousand members of the Chinese Academy of Social Sciences (CASS), whose building is

We do not want to live under bayonets.

just to the west of Jianguo Gate. I introduced myself, told them I was an American scholar of Chinese literature staying at Beida, and members enthusiastically asked me to walk with them in their demonstration. "You belong with CASS, right?" one said, making me feel like I was joining up with a group of old friends.

One man carried a sign reading, "We do not want to live under bayonets." Other slogans were, "Bury the cult of the individual and put an end to government by old men," and "Let all citizens rise up together and crush the military *coup d'etat*."

As we passed the CASS building, I noticed a statement written on a row of panels stuck along the front gate, each character on its own two-foot-square panel. "All citizens have the right to discuss (or criticize) the government. Supporting the students is not making a disturbance."

So the march began, and I walked with the CASS contingent in a demonstration of one million people, according to figures in the next day's *China Daily*. And what a walk it was! For me, it lasted from 1:45

*"Bury the cult of the individual and put an end to govern-
ment by old men. Let all citizens rise up together and crush
the military coup d'etat."*

till just after 4 P.M. We hiked from Jianguo Gate west and passed
Tiananmen, then turned around at Nan Chizi and walked back toward
the square. People came out of the homes and shops to wave and
applaud. They cheered each time the marchers chanted a slogan.

Along the route we had some serious discussions and we laughed
a good deal. One of my fellow demonstrators told me seven retired
generals had made a public statement against the policy of martial law
and military control.

Part of the way I read the *Asian Wall Street Journal*, which had an
editorial about China becoming part of the global village because of
the intense media coverage of the Democracy Movement, as well as its
recent acquisition of computers and fax machines. The editorial foresaw
only two possible future paths for the country: it could continue to
accept western technology and ideas, and the inevitable democratization that would come with them, or it could slam the doors like Iran

or Rumania, where the rulers would rather let their people starve than change the traditional way of life or risk losing power.

One of my fellow marchers borrowed the paper for a few minutes, then asked me to give it to him. I promised to make a photocopy and mail it to his office. The paper cost three *yuan* compared to a few pennies for a Chinese newspaper, so my friend couldn't afford to read it regularly.

The group chanted many different slogans all along the march. It may seem ridiculous since this was an illegal demonstration anyway, but I didn't shout their slogans. I felt it was not for me, a foreigner, to say what they were saying even though I agreed completely. They shouted, "Oppose dictatorship, Li Peng resign!" and "Oppose military rule, give us back (Zhao) Ziyang!" A double entendre, "Clean up the garbage, labor donated!" was greeted with peals of laughter. By "garbage" they might mean the trash littering the square—or they just might be referring to the leadership of the Communist Party, in which case "labor donated" took on a special meaning.

"If Li Peng doesn't resign, we'll come back every day," they shouted. "Long live democracy, the people will win!"

Halfway through, I ran into an old friend who was walking the other way on the sidewalk looking for somebody. He saw me first and roared out, *"Hei! Du Maike!"*–my name in Chinese. We grinned like a couple of kids raiding the cookie jar and gave each other a big bear hug. It was a wonderful way to meet after almost two years, but we had no time to talk. Instead, we made a date to have dinner later.

I also ran into a former student of mine who said he was looking for a literary contingent where some of his friends were marching. Ever since the demonstrations began he had been sleeping during the day and staying up all night roaming the square with a Dare to Die Brigade, "looking for trouble"–protecting the square against surprise attack by the army or riot police.

As we passed directly in front of Tiananmen, a murmur went up from the crowd. I looked over just in time to see the gigantic picture of Chairman Mao splashed with ink. Some of the younger people around me thought it was a good idea, but most of the CASS contingent looked worried. They didn't want to give the government any further reasons to crack down on the movement.

The sky was clouding over as we reached Nan Chizi and shortly after we turned around the wind began to blow. Light rain fell for about ten minutes as we walked east along the Avenue of Eternal Peace toward the square. When we turned the corner in front of the Great

Hall of the People and headed south in the direction of Qian Men, the "Front Gate," one of Beijing's famous thunder storms hit us with the full force of its driving rain. As the rain poured down and we walked bravely on, the young and the old intellectuals of the Chinese Academy of Social Sciences, so often persecuted by the Chinese Communist Party that many of them still belong to, began to sing "The International."

I shall never forget the surge of fellowship that swept over us that day as we linked arms and walked proudly around Tiananmen Square in a torrential downpour, singing "The International" in Chinese. "The International," that sad song of lost hopes, betrayed trusts, and broken promises, . . . *Zhe shi zui hou di douzheng*, "this is the final struggle." If it were only true.

Finally the rain was so hard that we were soaked to the skin and our shoes were filled with water. We just huddled together and kept moving, slogging through deep puddles. The students inside the square, who had been smiling and cheering to see the adult intellectuals out in force to support them, rushed out from under their makeshift tents. They handed us umbrellas and pale blue and green plastic raincoats, but we ran over and handed them back, shouting thanks and *nimen geng xuyao*, "You need them more than we do." Obviously, they were going to live in the square through rain and blistering heat.

We sloshed along like that for ten or fifteen minutes, and then everybody started dashing for whatever cover we could find. My clothes were soggy, my shoes were full of water, and I was getting cold. How the hell was I going to get to my bicycle four miles away at Jianguo Gate, and then make the ten-mile trip back to Beida?

Just then a taxi came by and I asked for a ride. The driver and his girlfriend took me back to the Jianguo Hotel for free because I was part of "the movement." After ducking into a lavatory at the hotel to change into a relatively dry shirt (I always carried a spare long-sleeved shirt for protection against the sun), I talked with some of the staffers. Of course, they supported the students.

I found a taxi to take my bike and myself back to Beida. The rain had stopped, and the cab was caught up in the reassembled demonstration. The driver had another fare he'd arranged to pick up, so he let me off at the Friendship Hotel. I had to pedal the last twenty minutes to Beida. I made it back in high spirits to a hot bath and a cold beer.

After dinner, I watched the evening news on CCTV. The government network reported that Beijing was 80 percent back to normal, and showed a ten-second view of the demonstrations. The snippet made it clear that this was a huge march and not the work of a "very very small group of people" as President Yang Shangkun had claimed earlier. He had thrown in an extra *ji*, "very," in imitation of Cultural Revolution rhetoric.

The defacement of Mao's picture was played up, and the alleged perpetrators were shown under arrest. But the reports never mentioned the fact that they were grabbed by students in the Democracy Movement and turned over to the police.

The news also didn't show any of the banners reading "Down with Li Peng" or report any of the similar slogans, but the journalists were obviously doing all they could to show the nation what was really happening in Beijing. They did not read any further martial law directives, but they reported that the armies surrounding Beijing had moved into temporary encampments.

In an interview with a People's Liberation Army officer, the soldier said the army had no "contradictions"—Maoist rhetoric for conflict—with the people. Meanwhile, the people were seated all around him, preventing his troops from moving in any direction. At the same time they were also feeding his troops, chatting with them, sharing cigarettes and water.

In many places—Shanxi, Hebei, even Lhasa in remote Tibet—party committees were meeting to "deeply study and affirm Li Peng's important speech." The TV anchors read that liturgical cant out as fast as possible without raising their heads to look at the camera. They often paused, it seemed deliberately, at the wrong places. Obviously the news readers had no respect for what they were mouthing. Earlier in the day, some of the CASS people had said this was the way the readers told everybody that what they were reading was bullshit. A few days later other friends told me the people at CCTV all hated to broadcast the government stories. They drew lots to see who would have to read them.

The demonstrations that were continuing in other cities got no mention on CCTV that night, except that in Shanghai there was a "dialogue" between students and representatives of city government. So anti-government protests were going on there too.

At the Free Speech Triangle next morning, I noticed the student who had made me laugh two days before by shouting "Protect Zhongnanhai." He was standing around eating breakfast out of his metal bowl—a couple of steamed buns and some pickled vegetables. His blue jacket was covered with dust, there were dark sweat blotches under the arms, his formerly white shirt was nearly black, and his eyes were bloodshot.

"Well, did you save Zhongnanhai?" I said.

"You bet!" he said with a wry smile and a twinkle in his eyes. He said he had not slept for about 40 hours, and had been out at "the front" talking to the soldiers. Although he was exhausted, he was eager to talk. He told me what he was studying in school, and said he hoped to go overseas for graduate school. Besides his technical field, he was also an artist, he said—"I'm an artist," just like that, without the slightest trace of modesty. "You should come over and see some of my work someday."

I told him I studied contemporary Chinese literature, and he said he read a little when he had time, but that he was a good friend of a famous writer whose works I'd briefly written about. "You ought to come over. I'll introduce you to him!" His enthusiasm was infectious and I liked him immediately.

Next I went to the nearby free market to buy some fruit. The free market, officially known as the Regional Agricultural Products Trade Center, is where farmers sell the produce they're permitted to grow for themselves after fulfilling any state quotas. As soon as I walked into the big building, which is about the size and shape of a hockey stadium, I was greeted by a loud, "Hey! Hey brother, you came back!" It was Xiao Luo (I'll call him), a peasant in his late 20s who had become a *getihu*. I bought all my pears and oranges from him in 1986-87, and also supplied him with a fair amount of FECs to buy foreign cigarettes. He greeted me like a long-lost brother, shaking my hand vigorously with his grimy, muscular hand. He dusted off a low wooden stool and insisted that I "sit down, sit down and jaw a while."

I complimented him on his good-looking watermelons, one of which was cut open to let customers see what they were buying. He laughed, sliced off several pieces, and handed them out to me and to a small crowd of fruit sellers who had gathered around his stall. "He's from America," he said proudly. *Women shi lao pengyou*, "We're old friends."

Xiao Luo took a plastic bag and started to fill it with oranges. "Here are some oranges and a watermelon too, I don't want any money! We're old friends. What are you doing back here? Did your wife come with you?"

"I'm here alone, came to get in on the excitement. What do you think of the student movement?"

He looked around at his peers. "We're all for the students. The

The sign draped over the Fuxing Gate street sign reads,
"The people will triumph, Li Peng must fall."

students can do things we can't get away with. We can get by under any government, right? Because we've always got enough to eat, but the students are in the right, they know what to do. Here, take another watermelon."

"No, no, no, I have to pay you."

We bantered for a few minutes, then he gave in and let me pay him twenty FECs for a watermelon and a bagful of oranges. Just before I left, he tossed a couple more oranges in. "Next time you need fruit, you come back here, OK?"

"Right."

In the afternoon I biked over to the Shangri-la Hotel to have lunch and read the newspapers. Chinese papers published the gist of the retired generals' letter against martial law. But along with it, they printed a government statement that the old soldiers "did not understand" the real situation.

At two o'clock I rode to Tiananmen Square. This time as I pedaled past the five kilometer marker at Fuxing Gate Overpass, I noticed a cloth banner had been draped over it, reading "The people will triumph, Li Peng must fall."

There was a large crowd in the square. I walked around for a while, talked with students and listened to speeches coming over a loudspeaker above the Monument to the Revolutionary Martyrs, where the students had their headquarters.

As I walked off to the northeast, heading for the Peking Hotel, I heard a statement read from a group that called itself the Capital Intellectual Community. Addressed to the "People of the Entire Nation," it was an attack on Li Peng and the government's mishandling of the Democracy Movement. It said the movement's only aims were to oppose corruption and dictatorship, and strive for democracy. It blamed the government for the present dangerous situation because of its illegal declaration of martial law. There was no disruption of normal life in the city, the statement said, so there was no excuse for martial law.

The speech concluded by asking all Chinese people to:

—carry on the movement. "If we do not achieve our goals, we will not quit."

—insist that martial law should end immediately because life was perfectly normal in Beijing.

—call for the National People's Congress or its standing committee to immediately meet and veto the April 26 editorial in *People's Daily*.

—push for Li Peng to be stripped of all his party and government offices.

—urge the government to end its control of the news media, allow civilian-owned newspapers, and promote openness.

—urge the government to continue and broaden its reforms.

"The road to democratization is a long one," the group declared. Nevertheless, the journey had begun and "the last bastion of the dictatorial monarchy is about to be blasted into dust by the angry shouts of the people. Long live the people! Long live the Republic!"

I swung by Wangfujing, the main shopping street in central Beijing, which runs north and south past the Peking Hotel, and browsed around in the New China Book Store for a while. Business was perfectly normal. I left the store and walked north several blocks along the street from the intersection of the Avenue of Eternal Peace to the Foreign Languages Bookstore. Hundreds of people were reading the many anti-government essays, poems, and cartoons on the posters that were pasted up everywhere.

As I pedaled west from Tiananmen that afternoon in rush-hour bicycle traffic, I overheard two men beside me animatedly discussing the movement and the power struggle in the party's top ranks. In their early 30s, wearing tailored suits, they looked like either mid-level government functionaries or the executives of a semi-private corporation. In either case, they seemed to know what was going on. I asked them if there were any new developments at the top, and they said it would soon be announced that Zhao Ziyang had organized a "counter-revolutionary clique."

Wo de tian, "Good Lord, who would believe that?"

"It doesn't matter who believes it, nobody believes it; what matters is who announces it." Then they pedaled away furiously with their coattails flapping.

I turned up Sanlihe Road. A block away, a crowd of about 30 people had gathered around a pedicab parked beside the road. Young workers in dirty blue uniforms were discussing something heatedly. I stopped to listen, and gradually pushed toward the center. The young men noticed me, and when they determined that I understood Chinese, they asked me what I thought about the demonstrations. I told them I supported the students' efforts to establish democracy. Then the workers got down to party-bashing. Everybody agreed that those m_____ f_____ bastards deserved to be thrown out on their ears, but they had all the power.

Zamen, said one of the young men, employing the Beijing dialect's "inclusive we" that effectively made me part of the family, "We don't have anything but our bare hands. And you, a foreigner talking like you do with people like us, you better be careful."

"Thanks, I will, you better take care of yourselves, too. So long."

§§§

I went to the Student Broadcast Station on Thursday morning and learned that the United Association of Beijing Intellectuals was calling for a demonstration at 1:30. The group's organization was announced only the day before, when it issued a number of manifestoes. The statements were also read over loudspeakers at the square and distributed as leaflets at Beida and elsewhere around the city. From the general tenor of the statements, I gathered the group to be a sort of unofficial, autonomous version of the Chinese Academy of Social Sciences.

The *Hong Kong Standard* and the *International Herald* were the only papers available that day at the Shangri-la Hotel, where I had a buffet lunch. I did not have to pay for them because the clerks didn't really care about collecting money. Three of them asked me what the western press said about the situation in China, and I said many articles were reporting that Li Peng would be asked to step down. Nobody I talked with in China thought that was true.

United Association of Beijing Intellectuals march.

I rode to the CASS building to go on my second "walk with a few friends" to Tiananmen Square, finding fewer people than on Tuesday, and none of them were in the contingent with which I had walked before.

For two hours I marched in this demonstration, which was relatively small at only 300,000, according to the next edition of *China Daily*. I stayed with one department's contingent, led by a famous scholar whom I had wanted to meet for a long time. Wearing a red baseball cap, he was walking along under a red banner at the contingent's head. I introduced myself to him and arranged to interview him so we could discuss the contemporary scene sometime in late June. We expected this particular wave of student demonstrations would end by then; that is, after the proposed June 20 meeting of the National People's Congress.

He told me the Yang-Li-Deng hard-liners "are soon going to announce that Zhao Ziyang was organizing a counter-revolutionary clique . . . but we don't care. We are simply going to demand what we want. We are going to continue to oppose military government." He used the word *junguan*, which means the military occupation of civilian organizations.

"If they impose military government, we will have no freedom of speech and no freedom of the press. The Democracy Movement in China is going to be extremely difficult, extremely difficult. It will be

*"The people will triumph," reads the banner for the CASS
contingent in the demonstration.*

a very long struggle. But these two or three years are extremely
important."

He was relaxed, confident; he joked and talked with some graduate
students who came up to report on developments around the city. This
scholar seemed certain that no matter what the hard-liners did, the
movement would not end.

It was very hot, so I left the demonstration early and headed back
toward the International Hotel to pick up my bicycle. On the way I
encountered another parade, this one made up of several thousand
waidi, or "outside Beijing," students. They were a ragtag bunch, dirty,
crude-looking, but determined young people. Most were in their teens.
Carrying banners that identified themselves as from schools in Hebei,
Henan, Shanxi, Shaanxi, and elsewhere, they smiled and laughed.
Watching these young people file by toward Tiananmen for half an
hour, I felt a mixture of wonder and sadness. How is the Communist
Party ever going to control these kids? I thought. They'll grow up
remembering the heady days of chanting "Down with dictatorship,
Li Peng step down! The people will triumph! And long live democracy!"
Even if they didn't know exactly what democracy meant, they damned
well knew what dictatorship was and how much they hated it.

Back in the Shaoyuan, I listened to the radio while bathing, and
watched CCTV evening news while I ate my usual dinner of peanuts,

watermelon and beer. The doubletalk on the state media was thick enough to cut with a knife. Order had returned to life in Beijing, but the martial-law orders had not been implemented anywhere, despite all the praise for the People's Liberation Army. The peasant boys from Lanzhou in the far west and Mongolia to the north were sweating it out in camps all around Beijing while the party leaders fought over what to do next. As an article in the *Asian Wall Street Journal* said a day or so earlier, the government cannot win now. No matter what the officials do, yield to the demands or crush the students, they have been discredited in the eyes of the people.

Li Peng was shown meeting with three new foreign ambassadors, in public for the first time since declaring martial law. He tried to lecture them into believing that a small group of conspirators was behind all of the events in Beijing this spring. He gave them a lesson in the art of translation, saying that *jieyan*, "martial law," and *junguan*, "military rule," are different things in the Chinese language even though they were both being translated as "martial law" in the West. CCTV news did not use the usual voice-over for this bit of Orwellian doubletalk, a linguistic discourse that would have made Stalin proud of this 1950s Moscow-educated engineer. Listening to him talk and watching his facial expressions, I was reminded of the cab driver's comment, "How could he be premier?"

Li Peng was obviously no intellectual. Used to being pampered by a horde of underlings, he was ruthless and capable of all manner of evil. It seemed to me that he had thrown in his lot with President Yang and the rest of the Gang of Elders who ruled China. With no real power base of his own, this "most hated man in China," as the students called him, could be expected to show no mercy to his opponents. I thought, Li knows well that if he falls he'll be in grave danger of being torn limb from limb like the Italian Fascist he so perfectly resembles.

Tonight at the Student Broadcast Station there were many rumors about the troops: they had been stationed in the subways; they were in secret underground passages below the Great Hall of the People at the edge of Tiananmen; they were in the grounds of the Forbidden City; they were, of course, in Zhongnanhai, the top party members' living quarters.

It was also said that Zhao, Defense Minister Qin Jiwei and Politburo Standing Committee member Hu Qili had been placed under house arrest. Zhao's children were said to fear for his life. Some regional army commanders had been dismissed for their reluctance to follow orders, and one of them committed suicide. Outside troops had been called in (I thought everybody knew that already). Fang Lizhi was arrested. Vice Premier Wan Li was under house arrest—or, as it was put, "in the hospital"—in Shanghai. All of Zhao's "brain trust" advisors and many other liberals would be arrested soon. The number of delegates calling for an emergency meeting of the National People's Congress had grown to more than 50.

About 10,000 students who were still occupying the square were debating their next moves, the loudspeakers said. Some suggested they should leave but most were for continuing their sit-in. They had been joined by a large contingent of young workers from the newly formed Independent Worker's Union.

Everybody knew the occupation was dwindling. Meanwhile, the students and townspeople had started a strategy called *san banr dao*, "three troop rotation." In order to avoid becoming too exhausted, one group would be on duty at the square or out propagandizing the troops while two other groups would head back to campus and rest. That way, they figured they could keep up the struggle indefinitely.

I knew the Chinese government was preparing to hurt the people again, but in the end it seemed they couldn't win. The people's mood of non-cooperation was much stronger than when I saw it in 1987. Of course, many people, like some middle-level cadres I had come across, would do what they've always done—take any action needed to survive. But many others even inside the party would push for an end to corruption and an increase in freedom.

§§§

Friday morning, a BBC journalist said a "usually well-informed source" told her most of the rumors that I had heard at the Student Broadcast Station the previous night.

This morning two extremely interesting posters were put up at the Free Speech Triangle. Both were written by older intellectuals, almost certainly professors who were Communist Party members. They were signed by pseudonyms.

"One Stone" wrote the longer one, which was entitled, "1989 Declaration." It was a passionate plea for the intellectuals and the party to support the people's struggle.

"Chinese society has experienced tremendous changes as it stepped out from a slough of turmoil. All we ever long for is stability, but we are destined never to escape from turmoil and disturbance. This seems to be the perversity of history.

"Why have things turned out this way? Because we have not yet washed ourselves clean of the filth and shame of the past. Corrupt thoughts and perverse behavior still persist into the present. Because the will of the people is still being violated and the Republic is still being disgraced. Because the great Chinese Communist Party has been turned into a tool that is arrogantly manipulated by a few individuals.

"The fate of one billion honorable citizens of the Republic is capriciously decided and willfully trampled upon without any regard for their aspirations. Is this our ancestral homeland? No! I would rather be a refugee with no nationality wandering dispossessed and in exile in a foreign land. . . ."

The next section of "One Stone's" essay was a confession that the older members of the intelligentsia had remained silent too long before joining the 1989 Democracy Movement. "Why did we remain silent? . . . It was because we have always been on our knees. . . . We shall not keep silent again!"

The third section examined the many ways in which the Communist Party leadership has betrayed the interests of the majority of Chinese. It was also a statement of the awakening of the party-member intellectuals to the true nature of the party. "In the last few years the party and the government have gradually revealed their true nature. We have gradually come to a much clearer understanding of the present state of the party and the government. . . . The party has a future only if it resolutely represents the interests of the people." At present, he went on, it does not do so.

In the last line of his long poster he proclaimed, "Democracy, this is the declaration of the citizens of our Republic!"

The other important big-character poster to appear on May 26 was by "a Communist Party member who loves you and supports you and who once did a disservice to the people." Addressed to the university students, it asked them to please think carefully.

The students must beware the government's cudgel, its anti-bourgeois liberalization campaign, he urged. The writer reminded the students of the way Mao promised there would be no reprisals for political criticism, a trick to "entice the snakes out of their holes" so he could crack down on all the intellectuals who dared speak up. "The past is a lesson for the future. Whatever you do, you must study our past history well."

During the Anti-Rightist Campaign of 1957, of which Deng Xiaoping was a principal leader, more than 700,000 people were persecuted as rightists. Although the party re-evaluated the campaign in the late 1970s and early 1980s and decided it was excessive, the necessity for such a campaign was never repudiated.

The Maoist method of controlling the intellectuals must be completely rejected, the writer argued. Deng must not be allowed to continue using the label "bourgeois liberalization" to attack all genuine reformers. To accomplish their goals, the students should pick up on the strategies of Mikhail Gorbachev. The Soviet leader couldn't be considered a bourgeois liberal. So Gorbachev's proposals could be used "to fend off Master Deng's cudgel. . . ."

"We can use Gorbachev's speeches as supporting arguments. In order to avoid being attacked, you should quote Gorbachev's speeches as much as possible; don't quote the speeches of bourgeois scholars. We have to use our brains in order to successfully carry out this battle to defend human rights."

The writer pointed out that the Chinese Constitution gives the elected representatives in the Beijing City Congress the right to dispose of a tyrannical government. Students should exhaust every legal means to attain their goals, while stressing Gorbachev's call for *glasnost*, or openness in government.

"Gorbachev's openness is a magic mirror that reveals all the evil demons. We must fight to have the National People's Congress legislate such openness." Only then can the various "black hands" that protect corrupt officials be revealed and their evil deeds prevented, he said.

The students must continue to pursue every possible public scrutiny of government officials, he added.

"These are heavy burdens, but determined young people have to think and study carefully. The danger we face is too great. The weight of China's future rests upon your shoulders. If you do not exert every ounce of your strength, it will certainly crush you to death!"

"Children, why have you shaved off all your whiskers?"

"Mama, we listened to Li Peng's report and we're all afraid!"

CHAPTER 5

ONE SENTENCE

DURING A SLOW BICYCLE TOUR OF DOWNTOWN BEIJING on Saturday, May 27, I noticed an enigmatic cartoon posted at the intersection of Wangfujing and the Avenue of Eternal Peace. It showed a big mother cat and a row of thirteen kittens. Mama looked normal, but the kittens had no whiskers. "Children, why have you shaved off all your whiskers?" the mother asked in the caption. The kittens replied, "Mama, we listened to Li Peng's report and we're all afraid!"

It would be interesting to know whom the cartoonist had in mind as the little cats. Maybe they were the political and economic reformers Deng Xiaoping mentioned a few years ago; he said the political color of these cats didn't matter, so long as they could catch mice. Now that the crackdown was on its way, many of them were said to be running for cover rather than standing up for their principles and supporting the students.

I stopped many times to talk with people on the streets or to photograph big-character posters. The signs were pasted up everywhere, on utility poles and walls, even inside most of the glass-enclosed newspaper display cases. So people in authority, with keys, were letting demonstrators put their propaganda inside.

Free Speech Hour at Beida was lively that evening. A defiantly tremulous woman's voice read out a dangerous poem that was both a riddle and a warning. It held the audience spellbound:

> There is one sentence,
> Spoken aloud it brings calamity.
> There is one sentence,
> That can cause a conflagration.
> Don't divulge it!
> Youth did not disclose it.
> You can understand
> Our silence deep as a volcano.

> Perhaps we'll suddenly be possessed,
> Lightning suddenly strike from the sky,
> *Our* China be born from the thunder!
> How's that, how can I express it today?
> It's all right if you don't believe an iron tree can
>   still blossom.
> But
> There is one sentence, just listen:
> Like a volcano that cannot bear the silence,
> Shakes its head, sticks out its tongue, stamps its
>   feet,
> When lightning strikes from the sky,
> *Our* China will be born from the thunder!

The sentence that youth did not disclose, though undoubtedly many thought it, was *Dadao gongchandang!* "Down with the Communist Party!" China may be an iron tree, the poet says, but we, the university students and young workers and common people are the buds that can make it blossom again.

An ominous poster written in gold paint with characters three inches high was tacked to the bulletin board in front of the Peking University post office. "Emergency Announcement," it began.

"According to absolutely reliable information, Party Central has already undergone very important personnel changes. The forces of reform have been seriously weakened. The situation is extremely grave and something unexpected is likely to occur. In order to protect the lives of the vast majority of patriotic students, to preserve our strength, and to securely safeguard the future development of democracy, (I) earnestly appeal to everyone to go to the square and persuade the students to return to school, explain the true situation, and understand clearly the present circumstances."

A major story on the Student Broadcast Station was that Deng had told his supporters that China would have martial law for many years, as long as any uncontrolled area remained. Also, despite indications that some members of the Politburo would like to end martial law in order to receive an important loan from Japan, the Yang-Li-Deng clique would not allow it.

On the loudspeakers, students reported that the Beijing Military Zone had now agreed to allow the enforcement of martial law. Presumably that meant that a settlement was made with officers who were opposed to the military repression of the Democracy Movement. It was a frightening report.

But the students remained brash and full of good humor in the face of the increasingly threatening situation. A satirical poem, "The Grand Chorus," poked fun at nearly every level of the government.

> The people ceaselessly questioned:
> > Why do we have absolutely nothing?
> The Consultative Congress sang out:
> > We love your songs but we're afraid to sing,
> > Whisper orders, furtively glancing left and right.
> Party Central sang out:
> > Hand in hand with Deng Xiaoping
> > We follow our emotions.
> > Our footsteps growing soft and dainty,
> > Our feelings warm and gentle.
> The Military Commission sang out:
> > With swords slashing off the students' heads,
> > Charge 'em! Kill 'em!
> The State Council sang out:
> > I'm a wolf from out of the far north,
> > Prowling the boundless wilderness.
> The National People's Congress sang out:
> > We only dream about our ancient land,
> > Power is something we've never had.
> The Provincial Government sang out:
> > When the moon comes out so do I,
> > Strolling with Old Deng down to the bridge.
> The County Government sang out:
> > It makes no difference what they sing,
> > > airs of the Southeast,
> > > airs of the Northwest,
> > They're all my songs, my songs.
> The Organized Township Government sang out:
> > I don't know
> > I don't know
> > I don't know
> > Which one's more perfect,
> > Which one more wonderful.
> The People sing out:
> > Down with Li Peng! Down with Li Peng!
> > Resist military rule! Resist military rule!
> > We demand democracy! We demand freedom!
> > And liberation! And liberation!

Peals of laughter greeted each of the allusive stanzas. For example, several lines are titles of songs, both by mainland and Taiwanese singers.

"I'm a wolf from out of the far north" is a line from a popular Taiwan song, "The Wolf." In this case, the wolf in the state council was Premier Li Peng. This song is said to be the one played most often on the square because it expresses the young peoples' powerful feelings of discontent. There was black humor in the Military Commission's verse, changing the line "Japanese devils' heads"–from the most popular song of the war against Japan–to "students' heads."

A graduate student said that although in the power struggle between Zhao Ziyang and Li Peng, the students supported Zhao, still "there is no substantial difference between them." That is, as party leaders neither believes in genuine democracy.

"Zhao Ziyang is really not our political ideal; his failure does not imply the failure of our movement. There is no reason to be pessimistic. China is still strictly controlled by a gang of old men. Zhao is not to their liking; even if there had been no student movement, he would have fallen sooner or later. So the responsibility for Zhao's defeat is not the students' but is to be blamed on the fact that dark conservative forces are still very powerful in the Chinese political arena."

The purpose of the movement, he said, was to awaken a new democratic consciousness throughout society. "From that point of view, we have achieved our projected goal. It was not our original intention to embrace any particular leader."

Another speaker announced that a big demonstration was being arranged for Tiananmen the next day. It would be a "demonstration of the world Chinese community" in hopes that Chinese in many other countries would hold simultaneous protests.

Meanwhile, students were hotly debating whether to leave the square. The arguments were complicated and confused, as is always the case with mass movements. An essay broadcast on the Free Speech Triangle at this time said, "If we leave the square now, we will be atomized by military control of the universities. We will be cut off from the people of Beijing. We will be secretly persecuted and punished, and we will not have achieved any of our major goals. We must not abandon the symbolic center of the movement."

That evening CCTV reported that Chen Yun, the 84-year-old chairman of the party's Central Advisory Committee, a hard-liner who was considered an expert on economics, was joining with the rest of the octogenarian Political Advisory Committee to voice full support for martial law.

"All the Chinese of the world unite!" reads a poster being prepared for the demonstration on May 28.

§§§

Sunday morning, the Voice of America claimed that the demonstration that day would mark the students' exit from Tiananmen Square as part of a victory celebration. This puzzled me, as the Student Broadcast Station hadn't said anything about leaving. But perhaps some wanted to step back and continue the struggle in other ways.

At 10:30 I biked down with the Peking University Bicycle Brigade to join a demonstration. On the way I struck up a conversation with a student who had participated in the hunger strike; one of his professors turned out to be a friend of mine. He agreed I could interview him whenever he had the time. All the way down Sanlihe Road, he talked enthusiastically about his hopes for the future when China would have a better government and he could concentrate on his field of study.

The demonstration was a small one, reported at about 50,000. Most of the protesters were students and many of them were from out of town. There were more onlookers than participants. Some demonstrators, especially the intellectuals, were depressed. People said a purge was underway in many work units. The public had access to all manner of Communist Party inside news by means of the Hong Kong and Taiwan newspapers that were photocopied and stuck up all

On the square, under the monument, the Propaganda Brigade prepares stencils for leaflets.

over town. The papers got their news, of course, from highly-placed sources who were willing to reveal "national secrets."

I made it into the hunger strikers' inner sanctum. On the third and highest level of steps under the Monument to the Revolutionary Martyrs, I spoke with members of their Propaganda Division and their Finance Committee. When I made a donation, a young man from the Finance Committee entered my name in a receipt book. I asked, only half-joking, if he didn't think he was helping the Public Security Bureau keep a record of "bourgeois liberals." He said the students wanted to know who their friends were for the future. Some people didn't want to sign, he said. But a French scholar told him the day before that he only wanted to sign it to let the party officials know he's against them and against their martial law. If a Frenchman signed, I thought, how could an American refuse? My name was entered for May 28.

The man from the Finance Committee said I was the first one to donate that day and he made me out a hand-written receipt. It read, "Received today from Du Maike, visiting foreign professor from Peking University, a donation of __ yuan RMB exactly. We are eternally grateful. Long live democracy! The people will triumph!" It was dated

I show the young man how to write my name in the ledger of "their friends" on May 28.

Receipt given to me on the square on May 28.

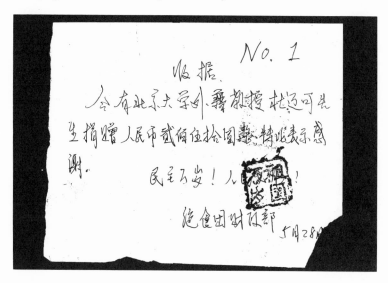

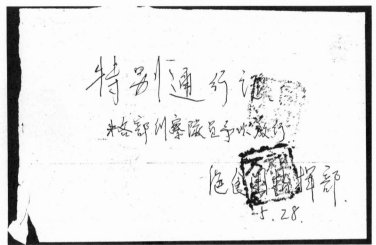

Special Transit Pass issued on the monument, May 28, in
Tiananmen Square.

and signed, "The Finance Committee of the Hunger Strike Group."
A red seal stamped it with the characters, "Long live the ancestral
homeland."

The whole ceremony was very touching. The quiet dignity and
determination of these sincere young people were unforgettable, as they
faced the state machine.

I was also awarded a pass written by hand on a piece of binder
paper. It said, "Special Transit Pass: to be granted entry by Public
Order Brigades of all units," and was signed by "The Directorate of
the Hunger Strike Group." I thought it would come in handy, as earlier
I had to do a lot of fast talking to make it through rows of stalwarts
from the Public Order Brigades who were trying to keep everyone but
hunger strikers and foreign reporters off the monument.

As I was looking around the square from the monument, I bumped
into my friend Edward Gargan, who was the *New York Times'* bureau
chief here from 1985 to 1987. We shook hands and he said, "I should
have known you couldn't miss this."

I was a bit embarrassed because I had not actually gone to China
to cover the movement. Gargan was on leave from the *Times* and had
a fellowship to write a book about the country. "Things are going to
get nasty here soon," he said. "All of Zhao Ziyang's people, everybody

I join with some boys from the Nationalities University on the square on May 28.

who knows how to make anything work in the economy, are going to fall."

Back at Beida later that afternoon, I had a visit from my former student who had been patrolling with the Dare to Die Brigade. He dropped around to my room to say good-bye, as he was on his way to the rural hinterland. He said most of the students from the Beijing campuses were going home now to avoid the violence that was coming. They knew they'd be safer in the provinces than in Beijing. By now, the majority of the students on the square were from outside the capital. They were joined by a large number of young workers from the newly formed Independent Workers Union.

The young man said that if the Gang of Elders who ran the country announced Zhao was the ringleader of a counter-revolutionary clique, there'd be a tremendous outcry.

I mentioned Gargan's prediction that violence would be used to clear the square. He said the students might not fight back, but the young workers he knew were quite ready for action: they wouldn't just sit there and let themselves be slaughtered. We agreed that the young workers hated the government more than anyone else because they had a hellish life even when employed. When they were unemployed it was worse. They had nothing to look forward to, and were ready to die if they could at least take "some of those bastards" with them.

Evening news on CCTV that night consisted primarily of readings from identical letters supposedly from the general public. They all called the students patriotic but asked them to trust the party and the government, and return to school. I thought this sort of coverage could have resulted from the fact that the media basically supported the students every way they could. Calling them patriotic might have been intended to protect them.

Then there were the videos of party meetings where everyone "enthusiastically supported" the government's policies. The identical statement was repeated half a dozen times. This was followed by admonitions from the official "labor unions" that workers must not strike in support of the students.

The news concluded with the usual parade of economic success stories, the reports that generally take up most of the newscast in normal times. Liu Binyan once remarked that this is the sort of thing that makes CCTV news one long bedtime story. Obviously, the leadership didn't have the votes to announce their "open secret" that Zhao is a counter-revolutionary, and they hadn't decided how to suppress the students.

At the Beida Broadcast Station that night, large crowds were listening to Hong Kong newspaper articles read over the speakers, reports about the inner workings of the Gang of Elders. Deng was going to officially denounce Zhao on May 29 or 30 and accuse him of many crimes, the papers said.

"As of this evening, the students have not left nor do they intend to leave the square until they are carried off by the police or the army," said one report. This statement gives some idea of what the students expected from the authorities. They expected to be dispersed in some rough but bearable manner by police and the army using standard crowd control tactics such as tear gas, water cannons, and clubs.

Some student leaders were now calling for a nationwide "movement of nonviolent noncooperation," in which people everywhere would boycott classes, stage strikes or slowdowns, refuse to buy state savings bonds, sell back bonds already purchased, and refuse to put money in the banks.

Many articles were read from *Xin bao* and other Hong Kong publications, saying the People's Liberation Army high command was still divided about what to do. The fact that troops were now camped outside Beijing for the eighth day without moving certainly indicated something—but what?

The students were debating about when to leave the square, according to the Voice of America's morning news on Monday, May

74

29. Should they go soon after the unveiling of the recently created Goddess of Democracy? Or should they stay until the meeting of the National People's Congress that was scheduled for June 20?

I bought a copy of a secret speech from students at Peking University—President Yang's May 24 statement to an emergency session of the Military Affairs Commission. It was tape recorded, leaked to the underground media, printed, and distributed throughout Beijing.

As a result of the present disturbance, Yang said, all the old comrades "agree that we have nowhere to retreat. If we retreat, we will fall from power, the People's Republic of China will be overthrown and capitalism will be restored . . . our socialism will become liberalism."

Speeches of other "old revolutionary comrades" in the government were published in the official newspapers and read on the CCTV evening news.

That afternoon I had to get my airplane ticket changed, and the process illustrates China's so-called modernization, and also may shed light on the way many Hong Kong businesses will be run after control reverts to China.

My ticket out was for August 25 on Cathay Pacific, a Hong Kong company, and I had purchased it in Vancouver. I took my voucher and the ticket to the offices of the Civil Aviation Administration of China (which everyone calls by the initials CAAC). I had to ask them to write a new ticket because China does not allow Cathay Pacific to sell tickets directly.

The clerk was as slow, dull and sullen as she could be. She studied my ticket for some time, scrawled figures on paper for a while, not even using a pocket calculator, then announced that my ticket was sold to me "too cheaply" in Vancouver. I would have to pay CAAC "too much money" for them to write it over. Suddenly she became friendly and offered a suggestion: I should go to the Cathay office and they could write a new ticket for me.

I raced over to Cathay Pacific, arriving at 4:30 P.M., only to be told they didn't have the right to sell tickets in China; they wished they did but they didn't. They told me the CAAC clerk had lied because "they don't know how to change a complicated ticket." They had another suggestion, that I should go next door to Japan Air Lines, even though they would lose my business in the process. Japan Air Lines has the legal right to sell tickets in China. Since the first leg of my journey had been on JAL, they would probably be able to change the whole thing for me.

In the denouement of this cautionary tale, two young Japanese with a computer modestly and politely ("Sorry to keep you waiting." "Thank you for waiting.") took twenty minutes to change my ticket from Cathay and Canadian Airlines to JAL's Beijing-Tokyo-Vancouver flight.

It will probably be a long time, if ever, before the Chinese in the People's Republic of China will be able to accomplish such a feat. If they persist in upholding the Four Cardinal Principles, that is. Chinese in Hong Kong, Taiwan, Singapore, Europe, and North America, where they are not hamstrung by the Chinese Communist Party's "socialist superiority," are every bit as capable of feats of modern efficiency.

At this time I was still planning to complete my literary research. I began filling out my application for a card at Beijing Library and bought a few books while I was downtown.

On two taxi rides, and in conversations with shop people today, everybody said the government was wrong about Zhao and there would be more trouble when the inevitable "official document" about him came down for all work units to study. It never came down until after the massacre. From then on, workers in every unit would be required to "unify their thoughts" by reading Deng Xiaoping's important speeches.

The *Asian Wall Street Journal* was speculating that Deng was going to drop both Zhao and Li Peng in order to preserve his own power. The story seemed to be based on a Chinese source privy to high-level information, maybe the same person who telephoned *The Nineties* in Hong Kong to give a detailed timetable for Li's exit.

Westerners in Beijing were saying that Deng's actions to date represented a terrible miscalculation by a man cut off from the mood of the people. A taxi driver summed it up for me: "After Deng dies, we will not respect his memory."

On CCTV news that night, Peng Zehn, the 87-year-old chairman of the Standing Committee of the National People's Congress, was lecturing the party's poor old "democratic" leaders about the need to support Premier Li and the Party Central. In an irony of Swiftian proportions, Peng said no one in China had the right to violate constitutional legality, as the students presumably had, and it is not permitted to practice "personalism" under the legal system. Personalism is the rule of persons rather than the rule of law. It is the main way the Chinese Communist Party runs the country. China's top leaders' ability to tell bald-faced lies without batting an eye never ceased to amaze me.

As always, the supposed democrats were reported vowing to cooperate with and support the Chinese Communist Party.

Wan Li, Chairman of the National People's Congress, who had been in Washington when the crisis started, wasn't boxed in at the Beijing airport after all. He was now in Shanghai, en route to Beijing. The CCTV English language news said he also had written a letter of support for the martial law policies.

And still there was no public attack on Zhao Ziyang. As yet, the leaders were not announcing what everybody knew they wanted to say about him.

§§§

I spent Tuesday reading leaflets, catching up on newspapers, biking, and doing what tourists do. I bought silk to be made into dresses for my wife, and small gifts to give in Vancouver.

Letters of support for martial law continued to be read on the CCTV evening news. The network broadcast views of entertainment for the troops stationed outside the city.

Letters were read from an architect in Beijing, and others, protesting the erection of "the statue of some goddess" on Tiananmen Square. One of these purported letters declared, "This is not America, this is China." It was intended to inflame anti-foreign prejudice, but ironically, everywhere I went people were happy to hear I was an American. They expected America to support their cause. For their part, the students were all too aware that they lived in China and not any western democracy.

The Student Broadcast Station said the demonstrators had debated whether to leave the square after the Goddess of Democracy statue was put up, but voted to continue their occupation. It also reported that this afternoon, police arrested three young workers from the Autonomous Workers Union and twelve members of a motorcycle club who were helping to protect the square. Hundreds of people were now surrounding the police station where they were held, and demanding their release.

An eyewitness told me they were grabbed on the street without warning, when they were not involved in any protest activities. A crowd quickly gathered. One of the workers was quick-witted: while scuffling with the police, he threw a small notebook into the crowd. It contained a list of names of people helping the autonomous union.

When people in the crowd saw what was in the notebook, they began to shout that the police were arresting leaders of the workers' movement. Then the crowd followed the police to the station and staged a sit-in, demanding the captives' release.

§§§

On May 31 I attended the monthly meeting of the National Academy of Sciences' Committee for Scholarly Communication with the People's Republic of China, the organization that gave me the fellowship to study there. The resident director for the 1988–89 academic year was Professor Perry Link, and the meeting was held in the Friendship Hotel. I was delighted to see an old schoolmate from Berkeley whom I had not seen in over ten years, and to meet scholars whose works I had read with great interest.

After a certain amount of cocktail conviviality, the meeting turned serious when one of the grantees suggested that we should write a letter to the committee executives in Washington protesting the Chinese government's mistreatment of both Perry Link and Fang Lizhi.

Link, a professor of modern Chinese literature, was being criticized by the leadership as one of the instigators of unrest. In February the Public Security Bureau prevented him and Fang from attending President Bush's farewell banquet, to which they had been invited. Subsequently, Link was harassed in the course of his duties as director of the committee. He was not allowed to attend a conference, and was refused permission to lecture in a class taught at a Chinese university by an American exchange scholar. Plainclothes police were following him and his wife wherever they went, and their telephone lines were tapped.

A government journal, *Weekly Outlook*, had published a false report about Link's relations with Fang Lizhi. The article claimed Link was some sort of an American government agent who had been dispatched to China to stir up trouble. Naturally, the journal refused to publish the rebuttal he sent.

Most of those present at the meeting agreed that the executive committee was far too lenient with the Chinese government over its interference with grantees, both American and Chinese. Many said the United States government should take a more active role in support of democratic reform in China. After an hour-long discussion, four of us volunteered to write the letter. We composed it over dinner and it was available the next day for the grantees to sign before it was sent to the executive committee in Washington.

All of the fellowship holders were certain a bad time was coming for Beijing's universities and research centers. I told them the Peking

University students were still active in the Democracy Movement, but they reported many smaller schools were already being strongly repressed by the authorities. People who used to talk to them were afraid to meet with foreigners now.

Grantees who had been there several months said I had missed the best time – the time when hope for change was highest. On May 17, they said, the protest march was one solid line all the way from Peking University to Tiananmen, more than ten miles. It included students, workers and every class of people. Some foreigners were so swept up with the excitement then that they thought the situation would develop the way Cory Aquino's "people's revolution" had in the Philippines.

My colleagues said the repression was beginning, but they believed the situation would always be better than it was before April 1989.

CCTV evening news continued its reports of party committees and central government departments announcing support for Premier Li and martial law. They showed pictures of a demonstration of 10,000 people on the outskirts of Beijing supporting martial law. The Committee for the Management of Tiananmen Square wrote a letter protesting the Goddess of Democracy statue. In one piece of good news, the Political Department of the Public Safety Bureau announced the release of the three workers arrested the previous day. No reason was given, but there was rumored to be resistance to martial law among the Public Safety Bureau officers in Beijing.

CHAPTER 6

INTELLECTUALS PREDICT TRAGEDY

I HAD A LUNCHEON INTERVIEW JUNE 1 AT A SMALL restaurant near the university, talking with the former hunger striker I met in the bicycle brigade. He was a skinny kid from the southwest studying in Beijing, cheerful, friendly, serious; his ambition was to be an academic success, and he had a deep foreboding about his country's future. He seemed a perfect example of the thousands of students who participated in the Democracy Movement that spring, with his easy-going lack of fear for personal safety and his matter-of-fact rationalism.

He enthusiastically described the inception of the movement with the simple requests that the negative criticism about Hu Yaobang be reversed after his death, and that the government send Premier Li Peng out to talk to the students about plans to overcome corruption, nepotism and inflation.

"Even the corrupt Beiyang (warlord) government sent someone out to meet with student protesters (in the 1920s), but this so-called people's government would not even talk to us," he said. "We sent three students up to kneel down on the steps of the Great Hall of the People, but they wouldn't even come out to meet with us." The gesture was like the kneeling that Chinese intellectuals and officials had to perform under the empire.

In the weeks that followed, he said, the student movement grew into a popular protest against government incompetence and corruption, coupled with demonstrations in favor of freedom, democracy, and political and economic reform. Now there was no turning back, he added. The declaration of martial law had revealed the true face of the ruling group.

Although they realized more troops were being stationed closer to Tiananmen and thought the army would sweep them off the square before the meeting of the National People's Congress in three weeks, many of the students were determined not to leave until they were "beaten up and jailed," the extent of the punishment they expected. It was a rational assessment, considering their youth, naivete and lack of first-hand experience with party cruelty.

This young man said he knew "for certain" that at least one hunger striker died during their fast. I asked him several times about that.

"He had a previous stomach disease that was made worse by fasting and he died," he said. "I saw him die. We didn't say anything though because the workers at the Capital Steel Factory had threatened to go on strike if even one student died. We didn't want to cause any more chaos, so we helped the government by keeping quiet about his death."

"You helped the government. Then you're not opposed to the Communist Party's leadership?"

"Well, it's not that simple. Some of us aren't, but most of us are. But we didn't want to openly attack the party. It would be counterproductive. Many party members support us and oppose the top leaders."

It was a long lunch, the restaurant was very hot, and I had to keep urging him to eat up. He was so thin I could hardly imagine him fasting for a week. In fact, he said the hunger strike had made him sick for several days afterwards.

Before he left he gave me a sheaf of leaflets and pictures of the demonstrators. Especially moving was a two-page photocopy of a picture of three students kneeling on the steps of the Great Hall of the People while a huge crowd looked on.

"Where are you?" I asked, pointing at the picture.

"I can't find myself in the picture, but I was there, and I'll be there next time too." We shook hands outside the restaurant, he thanked me for supporting the Chinese people, and I urged him to *baozhong*, "Take care of yourself."

I asked another student activist later in the day why so many students, possibly 3,000, were willing to risk their lives by joining the hunger strike. He said, "The students were ready to die because they've lost all hope in the future; they're in complete despair; they see little meaning to their lives and have little or no hope for the future, either for themselves or the country."

His words reminded me of a poem entitled, "The Call—dedicated to the hunger strikers." It was written by Fang Zhou ("The Ark") and posted on the wall of the Student Broadcast Station on May 20. It presents a touching expression of the sacrificial spirit of many student participants in the movement:

> People, people
> > We are not heirs of the dragon,
> > We are but grass
> > Growing on ancient and barren ground.
> > We are poor in money and status
> > Not in courage nor intelligence.
> Facing a long night with no dawn
> We offer up the torch of our lives.
> > Let this great ice-locked land thaw out
> > And Spring be more than just a fairy tale.
> > Let our grandchildren
> > Be born into equality
> > With no prenatal memory of poverty.
> Let the rain and dew of human integrity and rights
> Nourish you and me.
> May the emperors step down
> From off your necks and into the mud
> That you may stand up out of the mire.
> Motherland, fatherland
> > We are but grass
> > Not tiger cubs nor dragon children.
> We now contend against
> A storm surpassing our ability to suffer.
> > Hunger is a hawk
> > The burning sun a tiger
> > That tears at our breasts.
> > > If only my people
> > > Can escape calamity.
> > > If only you
> > > Can suddenly awaken from your torpor.
> > We have exhausted all our tears
> > Without once making you strong.
> > Perhaps our ashes
> > Can make you fertile.
> > We fall one by one
> > To fill the dark abyss.
> > If only my people
> > Walking across my body
> > Climb over the peaks of ignorance and poverty
> > To greet the light of our dreams.
> Friends, friends
> > If I fall

> Please tell my weary Mama
> Tell her not to weep.
> If I fall
> Please run and tell my brother
> Tell him to quickly take my place.
> If I fall
> Please don't remove
> My lettered headband.
> Youth's Spring is so lovely
> Bright blooming in May
> Sere and dead in May.
> The tombstone is so large.
> Among the names numberless as stars
> You will find me
> There eternally waiting
> Waiting for your graceful footsteps
> Following the flowers of May.

That evening I had an appointment to meet a group of people for dinner at a downtown restaurant. On the way, the taxi driver told me in his work unit a document had already come down from Party Central demanding that all drivers who participated in the Tiananmen demonstrations confess to their leaders at once. If they did, the government promised to be lenient with them. If they didn't and were subsequently turned in by informers or spotted in police surveillance photos, they would be summarily fired.

He and all of his buddies (*ge'r-men* in the Beijing dialect) had gone to the demonstrations and helped the students. After the edict came down, they met and agreed they could never trust the Communist Party's promise of leniency. They all decided to report they had never had anything to do with the demonstrations. He said his wife, an office worker, had received a similar ultimatum in her work unit.

Undoubtedly this was going on everywhere, and was the reason fewer people were marching now. The cab driver said he wished the Chinese people were armed. If they were, he said, the party would get what was coming to it.

My friends and I spent six hours talking in a restaurant and a tourist hotel's coffee shop. They were a good cross section of the Beijing intellectual, literary and artistic community. There was also a mid-level executive of one of the semi-private corporations. They were of both sexes and most were under 50. All were party members and some even held minor official or managerial posts in their work units. Most had good connections with at least one higher official or his immediate

83

subordinates, so they saw a great number of important documents and regularly spoke with people who saw even more and who attended high-level meetings.

The young business executive was leaving soon for Europe and this was sort of a going-away party for him. He had been active behind the scenes in support of the students, and we were all a little worried about his safety.

The person who had invited me introduced me with the words, "It's all right to talk in front of Du Maike." He added, *Ta shi ziji ren*, "He's one of us." It was an honor to be trusted by them.

We had a wide-ranging conversation, myself and these old friends who were used to getting together in times of crisis to share information and offer mutual support. I learned many things about the current climate and picked up even more inside information about the political situation. Although it's sometimes dangerous, one of the main things that makes life worth living for intellectuals in China's repressive society is the true friendship nurtured by this kind of trust.

Compared to American customs, the outward emotional expressions of such friendships are low-key. There's no embracing or kissing when they meet; sometimes they do not even shake hands. The traditional Chinese expression is *Junzi zhi jiao dan ruo shui*, "Friendship between men of honor is as bland as water." Nevertheless, deep feelings of loyalty and generosity among such buddies form a powerful bond.

Much of what they said about the current situation was frightening and disheartening. It was very bad this time, much worse than in 1987, they said. A set of Deng Xiaoping's political enemies, and the newly emergent Gang of Elders, would insist on killing many people.

"This time," one of them said matter-of-factly, "they are definitely going to do a lot of killing."

Another agreed, "Yes, they're going to do a lot of killing. They're out for blood this time."

"I think first they'll publicly execute a few criminals already in prison. Next they'll round up some leaders of every group that supported the Democracy Movement and execute some of them to terrorize the public," someone else said.

"Right," said another. The party would "kill some chickens to frighten the monkeys."

Among the groups whose leaders would be singled out for punishment they counted student organizations, the Autonomous Workers Union, members of motorcycle clubs, and many others, especially those few Beijing policemen who walked in the mass demonstrations of May 17 and 18.

They had solid information that the Commission on Restructuring the Economic System, a group of more than 100 professionals and experts closely associated with Zhao Ziyang's reform policies, would be disbanded and many of its members punished. They would not rule out executions for some.

They had it on "absolutely reliable sources" that Vice President Wang Zhen had gone to a meeting of this committee—or to a place where committee members were being held for questioning—and saved one of them who was a distant relative of his. He called the man out of the room, cursed him for associating with Zhao's reform group, and told him to make himself scarce before it was too late.

My friends debated what level of violence would be used on the students in the square. It was hard to predict, they said. It was certainly possible that tanks would be brought in as the Russians did in Hungary during the 1956 uprising. After all, they recalled, Deng Xiaoping had wholeheartedly supported the Soviet move at that time. They repeated a rumor I'd heard both at Peking University and among some townspeople, that Deng's policy was to "kill 200,000 in order to gain 20 years of peace." They didn't exactly believe it, but didn't dismiss it out of hand, either.

They agreed there would soon be some sort of violent suppression of the students, to be followed by a purge. Some discussed running away to the provinces where they came from, as they spoke the local dialects and had friends or relatives who could help support them. They could perform manual labor or work as "private entrepreneurs" for a while.

In the end, these often-persecuted intellectuals concluded that tanks would probably not be brought out because "we don't have that tradition in China." (From this we can gauge whether the students, who had even less experience of Communist Party ruthlessness, were irrational to remain on the square after martial law was declared.)

Some of them had been in the People's Liberation Army and had contacts with soldiers from certain regions. One said that so far, the troops in and around Beijing had not been issued ammunition. Some officers would no longer trust the common soldiers in their commands with ammunition unless it was absolutely necessary. The mistrust began in the 1979 war against Vietnam, in which many Chinese units were needlessly sacrificed. When they were ordered to advance against superior fire power in the old human-wave tactics used in the Korean

War, many units refused to fight such suicidal battles. Some turned their guns around and killed their own officers to exact revenge and to avoid moving forward to certain death.

Another fellow said that in recent years there were also incidents of infantrymen on guard during ceremonial occasions running out and gunning down officers on the stage. One he knew of personally: the soldier killed several officers and then shot himself.

The army was also fearful of demobilized soldiers, he said. When a large number are released at the same time, the usual practice is for them to be provided with a military escort back to their home villages. But in the present difficult economy, this usually meant being sent home to become unemployed. The discharged soldiers are extremely unhappy about this, and sometimes kill the officers who are escorting them. Junior officers in charge of such units have applied for assistance on numerous occasions. Recently, a county government on Hainan Island was held hostage for several days by a group of ex-soldiers clamoring for work.

Although none of this made headlines in the *People's Daily*, it was obvious to many Beijing residents that the army was fragmented to some extent. Units from one province would be loyal to certain leaders, and those from different areas would support others. This seemed to be part of the reason for the stalemate in the face-off between demonstrators and troops: party leaders weren't certain of their troops' loyalty, should an assault be ordered.

The friends believed that Defense Minister Qin Jiwei, Regional Military Commander Zhou Yibing, and many army officers had been removed from office—another indication of dissent within the military.

Concerning the pro-government demonstrations on the outskirts of Beijing, they said the government was paying peasants ten *yuan* each to participate, and was forcing work units to march along with them. They jokingly considered joining in too, then raising an anti-Li Peng banner and shouting democracy slogans at an appropriate time.

Most of the higher officials in charge of cultural responsibilities were refusing so far to support martial law, one said. All could be expected to be purged anyway because of their support for Zhao, so why not resist?

Reporters at the official New China News Agency had refused to work, refused to write stories that were only the outright lies of the government's propaganda, one of my companions said. The news was now being written by party hacks.

Liu Zaifu, director of the Literature Department at the Chinese

Academy of Social Sciences, and Li Zehou, the country's most famous historian of philosophy and aesthetics, plus many others, would certainly be in big trouble, they agreed. It was hard to estimate just how bad their trouble was or whether their lives would be in danger. When the purge of genuine intellectuals is carried out, they thought, the rulers would find some "cheap and shameless intellectuals" to speak on their behalf.

As we finished our beer and coffee, these people came to some discouraging conclusions: they sadly and stoically agreed there was no real hope. One said somebody had told him recently, "The party is hopeless, but there is still hope for the country." He disagreed with that. "But the truth is the country is hopeless too," he said.

First, these friends said, China's population explosion was continuing. Despite official attempts to control it, they estimated the population would not level off until it reached 1.6 billion, nearly half again as large as the present 1.1 billion. Further, the poor and ignorant were increasing much faster than the educated people.

Second, the party government is so corrupt and incompetent there's no rational reason to hope for improvements in the long run. They told hair-raising stories about the ignorance and incompetence of high party leaders, the same people who were asserting control over the factory managers, engineers and other trained technicians at most work places throughout the country.

Not only was China hopeless, but "anything can happen in China now," they said. They meant anything including civil war, an armed or unarmed insurrection, or Boxer Rebellion-type madness — any imaginable type of irrational calamity.

Before the group broke up, we walked to the square for a look at the Goddess of Democracy. Standing in front of the statue and looking behind it at the few thousand students still camped on the square, our group had a palpable air of nostalgia. It was an existential longing for something they were certain would soon be destroyed, for something that had scarcely come into being, for something utterly precious and intangible.

Riding my bike back to Beida that night, I felt a terrible weight of sadness to think that these committed intellectuals had such a dark view of China's future. Perhaps they were simply too close to their own troubles, too emotionally beaten down by their past experiences. I've met many other Chinese scholars who feel differently about the future. But then others, who were less emotional than my friends of this night, had told me there's little real hope for China to develop a strong, healthy political and economic life.

Perhaps they were wrong. Perhaps not.

June 2, my last view of the Goddess of Democracy.

CHAPTER 7

ON THE AVENUE OF BLOOD

A stray bullet hit me in the chest,
The past instantly streamed into mind,
There was no sadness, only tears.
If that was the last shot fired,
I gladly accept this greatest honor.
I wonder how many,
How many people are just like me.
I wonder how many,
How many last shots were fired.

Cui Jian

N ARMY JEEP RAN INTO A CROWD OF BICYCLE RIDERS near Muxidi Bridge, a few miles west of Tiananmen, on Friday, June 2. Three Beijing citizens were killed on the spot and one was hospitalized in critical condition. People were outraged. CCTV carried a special report of a hastily called news conference in which a government spokeswoman tried to explain that this had nothing to do with martial law. The driver was shown confessing his guilt for the terrible accident. The point of the exercise was to mollify public opinion, which was running high against the military presence.

Later that evening the Beida Student Broadcast Station* reported that four famous Chinese were joining the students on Tiananmen Square—Hou Dejian, a popular singer who left Taiwan for the mainland six years before; Liu Xiaopo, a young lecturer at Beijing Normal University, immensely popular with the students; Zhou Tuo,

---

*   Chapters seven and eight are based on eyewitness reports on Beida loudspeakers, interviews I conducted, and a number of published accounts, most of which I translated from Chinese. For a full list of quoted sources, see Sources and Acknowledgments.

head of the Stone Computer Corporation's Planning Division; and Gao Xin, a journalist. They said they regretted not joining earlier and announced they were going on a penitential hunger strike.

"The Chinese intellectual community must bring an end to its thousand-year-old tradition of spinelessly exercising our mouths but not our hands," said their statement. "We must take action to oppose military government, take action to support the birth of a new political culture, and take action to express our repentance for the mistakes caused by our long-standing weakness."

Some of the 150,000 to 200,000 troops surrounding Beijing attempted to jog toward Tiananmen on foot, but the Voice of America's news on Saturday morning said they were halted by 10,000 students, workers and Beijing citizens. Soldiers seemed on the move around the city. I thought government officials were either undecided about how to proceed, or had made some sort of a decision but were unable to carry it out.

I went to the Student Broadcast Station as usual. An eyewitness report on the jeep accident was broadcast, and a demonstration was called for 2 P.M. to protest the incident and demand an end to martial law.

At one o'clock I started toward Tiananmen with a contingent of Peking University bicyclists. When we approached Muxidi, a huge crowd was milling around where the accident happened, and I saw a burned-out army vehicle there. Approaching the Xidan intersection, traffic was snarled by a roadblock made of parked buses. I inched my bike east between a couple of them, as did hundreds of others who wanted to see what was happening farther down the road.

On the Tiananmen side of the blockade, a police vehicle—which looked like an unmarked family car, but people told me it was a police car—had been seized by the crowds. Young men sat and stood on top of it, none of them looking like students. Suddenly, from the direction of Tiananmen we heard the distant "poom poom poom" of tear gas canisters being fired.

It's started, I thought. I was moving back to take up a position on the west side of the bus blockade when I discovered my bicycle's back tire had gone flat. I stood in the street for more than an hour, taping interviews and watching and listening to the hubbub a few blocks ahead. Eventually I left my bike at the side of the road and started forward. Just then, several young men walked over from the direction of the disturbance.

One climbed onto the trapped car with a bullhorn and announced

The Xidan intersection at 2 P.M. on June 3.

that troops or riot police had rushed out in force at an intersection known as Liubukou, the first street west of the Zhongnanhai compound. They attacked the people with tear gas, clubs and rubber bullets, and retrieved a vehicle full of weapons that the crowd had seized earlier in the day. At this, furious shouts of "Bastards!" and "Beasts!" rang out all around me.

A few minutes later a young man walked proudly by carrying a tear gas canister high in the air for everyone to see. Another youth with a wet cloth around his neck, red splotches on his face, and eyes bloodshot from tear gas held up what he said was a rubber bullet. He held it high in his left hand while gesturing with his right fist and shouting angrily, "The army's firing rubber bullets at the people!" This was taking place just a few blocks closer to Tiananmen.

He came over to where I was talking with two older men who had just returned from the melee near the party compound. One was telling me, "This is the way the people's army treats the people!" I asked what they would like me to tell people back in North America, and one shouted with tears in his eyes, "Go back and tell the world exactly what is happening here in China!" A mild odor of tear gas wafted over from the east.

I asked a number of people what was happening near Tiananmen

Square, and many answered, incorrectly, that riot police and the army were sweeping the square clear with tear gas, clubs and rubber bullets. I returned to the Minzu Hotel—if the square was being cleared and the demonstrators arrested or driven away, there wasn't much use in trying to get a closer look today. I might as well go back to the university and see how the students were reacting.

Cab drivers refused to drive me to Beida, saying it was too dangerous. Troops were moving all around the city and there were bound to be clashes with the crowds. Someone might try to take their taxis, or they might get trapped in the middle of a violent confrontation. They couldn't afford to risk it. Then one said, "Old Zhang [not his real name], Old Zhang'll take you. He's not afraid of anything."

A middle-aged man who had lived through the Cultural Revolution in Beijing, Old Zhang said we could make it to the university by following Beijing's *hutongs* (narrow alleys), and staying off the main roads that were likely to be used by the army. As we were leaving, his fellow drivers yelled, "Be sure and pay him plenty extra when you get there!"

It was a bumpy but uneventful ride, and we drove close to thousands of front gates on lanes that were too narrow for more than one vehicle. It seemed as though everyone in the city was out trying to learn what was happening at Tiananmen. Thus I returned to Peking University, believing the army had finally been ordered to clear the students off the square by ordinary techniques of crowd dispersal.

I realized my mistake as soon as I switched on the CCTV news at 7 P.M. A strong warning from the Command Headquarters of the Martial Law Forces was repeated several times, ordering the people of Beijing to stay home and off the streets, and in particular, not to go to Tiananmen Square. If anyone interfered with the troops in the execution of their duty, as they had been doing for fourteen days now, they must take full responsibility for the consequences. It was obvious the army and police were going to clear the students and workers from the square that night, and they were prepared to kill anyone who got in the way.

The news also reported that Qin Jiwei, the defense minister who had been rumored to oppose martial law, visited officers and men of the Martial Law Forces to deliver greetings from Deng Xiaoping and President Yang Shangkun.

I hurried to the Student Broadcast Station. The loudspeaker had been moved to a much higher perch in another tree, and it was hard to hear. I continued over to the school's south gate, where student reports came over the loudspeaker detailing the seizure of the police vehicle and the army's attack on the crowds near the party compound.

A student said that in the morning, a large crowd surrounded a contingent of People's Liberation Army soldiers who were marching in formation toward Tiananmen Square. They were furious at the soldiers because they seemed to be preparing to drive the students away. They cursed the troops, pushed them around, and were on the verge of really hurting them when a group of student leaders forced their way between the soldiers and the crowd and calmed the crowd. They ordered the soldiers to throw down their arms and other gear, then lectured them about what was really going on in Beijing. They asked, Weren't they ashamed of coming here to attack the people who were engaged in a peaceful nonviolent protest?

The soldiers answered they knew nothing about that, they had simply been ordered to march in here and they had not been issued any ammunition. They didn't know what they were supposed to be doing. The eyewitness said the troops were terrified of the crowd. In the end, the students forced the troops to take off their army shirts and then helped them go back where they had come from, heading away from Tiananmen.

At about 8:15 a call came from the loudspeakers to go to Tiananmen and protect it from the expected invasion. Bicycle brigades began to stream out of the gate. They kept pouring slowly out of the Peking University campus for an hour. I recognized students, faculty families with children, and all sorts of people who live and work around campus. At 9:15 the loudspeaker announced, "There are now 200,000 people" on the square; that was considered enough to hold it and protect it through the night. Volunteers were asked to go to the roads that the army was expected to take into the city, and block the troops again.

These people are so brave in the face of overwhelming force, I thought. I only hope they don't needlessly sacrifice their lives.

Eyewitnesses told the crowds at the south gate about the jeep incident. At about 10:40 P.M. the day before, they said, a convoy of eight medium-sized jeeps carrying armed riot police headed toward Tiananmen at high speed, whipping along the Avenue of Eternal Peace. At Muxidi, the last jeep in the column suddenly veered to the right into the slow-vehicle lane and crashed into the driver of a three-wheeled pedicab. It plowed into two men on bicycles and ran over a woman pedestrian, then overturned on the sidewalk. A couple of hundred people, who had gathered to halt the army's advance, witnessed the incident. Many believed it wasn't an accident, but a deliberate attempt to stir up a riot.

An angry pedestrian, who was nearly run over by the jeep, pulled the driver out. The first thing the driver said was, "I was carrying out a mission. It's not my responsibility." The pedestrian then slapped him across the face.

At that point a jeep belonging to the Public Security Bureau, which had been traveling a short distance behind the police convoy, pulled up. Its driver radioed police headquarters to send a camera crew. People on the scene quickly loaded the injured into a passing car and sent them to Fuxing Hospital, a witness said. Two men and the woman died, according to another report. A third man suffered internal injuries, including a broken back, and probably was crippled for life.

The police camera crew finished photographing the scene and left. Then people organized themselves into a Public Order Brigade and wouldn't let anyone clean up the area. They yelled, "Look at this, everybody; look who's really causing a disturbance." Someone stood on the jeep and called on the crowd to rush to the hospital and guard the corpses. They intended to carry them through the streets in a protest march the next day.

People on bicycles left Muxidi and rode east on the Avenue of Eternal Peace shouting slogans like, "A debt of blood should be repaid in blood!" and "Down with Li Peng!" More joined the group, until over a thousand were riding along together.

Earlier that same afternoon of Friday, June 2, Yang Shangkun, Li Peng, Wang Zhen, Bo Yibo, Qiao Shi, and Yao Yilin are said to have met at Deng Xiaoping's home. At that meeting they made two fateful decisions: to employ military force against the students on June 4 and to change their interpretation of the Democracy Movement from a "disturbance" to a "counter-revolutionary rebellion." When Zhao Ziyang learned of their decisions, he telephone Yang Shangkun, Li Peng, and several other members of the Politburo Standing Committee as well as the retired generals Nie Rongzhen and Xu Xiangqian. He pleaded with them not to carry out the military suppression, but his pleas fell on deaf ears. That evening he actually decided to go on a hunger strike and continued his remonstrances. It was all to no avail. The military juggernaut had already been set in motion.

Sometime that evening, large numbers of troops were ordered to move quickly into Beijing. They clashed with townspeople throughout that day and Saturday. The first encounter was at about 3:15 A.M. directly in front of the Beijing Hotel. By then thousands of Beijing

95

residents were busy piling up metal street railings to prevent army trucks from entering Tiananmen Square. A long line of troops marched toward the square on the south side of the Avenue of Eternal Peace, in close formation, six abreast, their heads shaved, wearing olive-green pants and white T-shirts. Radio operators were spaced through the formation every 20 or 30 men. When they reached the corner of Zhengyi (Justice) Street, they were blocked by a large group of civilians.

Many of the people were called out of bed, and some were dressed in pajamas with blankets thrown over their shoulders. With ten or more on each end, they pulled up a rope hung with slogans, so it was in front of the soldiers, and yelled at them to go back. They shouted that the troops should not harm the students. Women wept and pleaded, saying such things as "Please go back! What do you mean coming to our homes?"

The soldiers were recruits, only eighteen or nineteen years old themselves. They were hot, dirty and tired. While this stand-off was taking place, several crumpled up on the ground. Each carried a small knapsack, two pairs of shoes (one pair leather, one pair plastic), and a plastic raincoat. They had no weapons. Some were moved by the arguments and began talking softly with the people. They said they were from Shunyi County, about 45 miles outside Beijing, and they'd marched since 1 A.M. to get there. An older woman cursed Li Peng for treating "these children" so badly. The entire contingent stayed there for an hour, then retreated east on the Avenue of Eternal Peace, to the cheers and applause of townspeople.

I heard of a similar incident on the loudspeakers at the university, early on the evening of June 3. The question is, why were these unarmed soldiers marched toward Tiananmen? Some soldiers were on the road four hours before they were stopped.

I think it was a deliberate provocation, intended to start a riot and provide an excuse to send armed troops to the rescue. At any rate, in both cases an explosive situation was defused by either students or townspeople. They are just two more examples of the nonviolent and rational nature of the popular movement.

A young woman named Mrs. Li, whose home is close to Tiananmen Square, was called from her bed before dawn on June 3 by neighbors who said the army was trying to enter the city. She rushed out with them to the Xidan intersection near the Zhongnanhai Compound, where a crowd had formed a human wall in front of troops said to be from the 24th Army. The soldiers stopped.

Later, Mrs. Li said, the people were shouting things like, "The students are not in rebellion! You've been tricked!" These soldiers were peasant boys about sixteen or seventeen years old who were normally stationed in Chengde, a day's train ride northeast of Beijing. Marched double-time all night, they were exhausted and confused by the confrontation. By daybreak they were restless and undisciplined. Xinyuan went home and dressed, then returned. The crowd was still trying to hold back the troop trucks when one of the trucks ran into three people, injuring an old man and killing two others. It was reported in the *Beijing Daily* as a traffic accident, she said.

While that was going on, thousands of heavily armed troops were entering the city. About 3 A.M., an emergency call came over the Tiananmen loudspeakers: troops had moved in behind the Great Hall of the People; they were stationed inside the Historical Museum. Armed soldiers were spotted on the street just west of the Beijing Hotel. There were vehicles transporting weapons on the West Avenue of Eternal Peace. By daybreak a large military force faced Tiananmen on at least three sides.

A rambling oral report was given to his fellow students by a *waidi* student (that is, one from outside Beijing), which was broadcast later on a Hong Kong radio program and published in the *World Journal.* At times his voice broke. I'll call him Hua (for Chinese), although that was not his name. He was a member of the University Students United Autonomous Association from Outside Beijing.

He said a "strange phenomenon" began June 3. A few trucks loaded with undisciplined troops would suddenly drive toward the square from Xidan. They would be stopped by crowds protecting the square's outer perimeter. Then the soldiers would immediately dash off, leaving their trucks behind. Students would climb into them and take the assault rifles and other arms. They didn't know what to do with them so they immediately brought them to the Autonomous Association headquarters. There, the leaders quickly broadcast a warning to all students not to fall into some kind of government trap—that the government might want people to think the students were engaged in an armed insurrection.

The guns were given to one of the student brigades to be handed over to the Public Security Bureau. Hua did not know if they were delivered to the police or not.

One eyewitness said the students tried to hand the weapons to various army units and the officers said they were not authorized to receive them. Democracy Movement participants believed this was the true story behind the government's evening news broadcasts that some hooligans had stolen military equipment.

Special agents were also sent in by the army. Hua said two companies of plainclothes soldiers came onto Tiananmen on June 2 and 3 while the Students Autonomous Association was holding meetings. They spread out and were hard to distinguish. Loudspeakers warned of their presence; the soldiers eventually departed, but left army shirts and hats behind. The students naively put them on and even took each others' pictures while so clothed. The government news later reported that rioters had stolen military uniforms, ammunition, etc.

"I saw all this myself," Hua said. "It was all a trap."

A Chinese woman who is married to an American college professor told a friend of mine that she unmasked several plainclothes soldiers on the square simply by the way they talked. When she said, "You're a soldier, aren't you?" they blushed and quickly walked away.

Students showed off captured military equipment from dawn until midday at several locations. At the Xidan and Liubukou intersections the crowd had stopped three large tour buses full of military hardware. These were the buses I saw blocking the Xidan intersection on June 3. The students piled up gear on the buses for everyone to see: machine guns, assault rifles, boxes of cartridges, hand grenades, rifle grenades, gas masks, helmets and walkie-talkies.

There was another display at Xinhuamen, the New China Gate behind which are the party headquarters and the Zhongnanhai compound where the leaders live. Here, students showed army shoes, hats, belts and knives. Many Beijing residents filed past to see this evidence of the army's unfriendly presence.

The bloodshed began at 2 P.M., just as I was arriving at Xidan with my disabled bicycle. People were looking at captured military equipment when a loudspeaker suddenly blared out a warning for the people around Liubukou to disperse immediately. Soon afterwards, about 1,000 soldiers, military police and traffic patrolmen stormed out of Zhongnanhai and formed into ranks on the West Avenue of Eternal Peace. They were a human wall with regular soldiers in the rear. An officer climbed on top of a jeep and shouted, "Carry out your mission now!"

Soldiers in the back shot off about twenty canisters of tear gas in the direction of the crowd. At the same time a group of soldiers and military police laid into the crowd with electric prods and wooden batons. People ran east, leaving a pile of bikes and personal belongings. At about the same time the identical scene was happening at the New

China Gate, where 300 soldiers were beating the crowd with prods and nightsticks, forcing students and townspeople back halfway across the Avenue of Eternal Peace.

Then the troops pulled back to the front of the New China Gate, refusing to let people back to where they had been sitting-in for several weeks.

More than 40 protesters were injured by clubs in the hour-long confrontations. The staff at Fuxing Hospital told a reporter for *Wenhuibao*, a Hong Kong publication, that a pregnant bypasser was beaten and suffered a miscarriage.

The purpose of the attacks seems to have been to retrieve the weapons. Authorities must have worried that somebody might use them. Both places are near Zhongnanhai, and the presence of weapons in the hands of hostile citizens there must have been frightening.

Why did other soldiers abandon the weapons in the first place? One possibility is that the government tried to plant them on the students, but then the demonstrators put them on display. Because the New China Gate and Liubukou are so close to Party Central and the leaders' compound, the government became frightened and decided to retrieve them before anyone put them to use.

That afternoon, there were many scattered incidents in which soldiers beat civilians. Crowds surrounded about 1,000 troops near the west gate of the Great Hall of the People and the soldiers clubbed them. Soldiers inside the walls, directly opposite the west gate, threw bricks at people outside the Great Hall. Traffic on the Avenue of Eternal Peace was blocked during these confrontations until about 6 P.M., when the troops on the west side of the Great Hall withdrew.

By then, several hundred thousand people were in Tiananmen Square. Some were there to watch the opening ceremony of a new "Democracy University" that the students planned for 10 P.M.; some were drawn by news of the conflict.

A young man who lives on the outskirts of Beijing told a friend of mine that on the night of June 3 he watched a column of troop trucks cross a bridge leading into the city. A group of students and townspeople halted the convoy. Troops standing in the trucks looked frightened and held their weapons at ready, but then realized the crowd only wanted to talk to them. The people said they were not in rebellion, and tried to explain what was really happening.

The company commander stopped his trucks and refused to go any farther, but it was hard to turn around on the bridge. One truck tried to turn and ended up blocking the bridge. Just then a tank from another unit roared onto the bridge, rammed the trucks with the troops in it, and pushed the truck into the river so the tanks could continue across. The company commander was livid, cursing, telling the crowd that if his men had been issued live ammunition he would have turned his guns on the tanks and taken his chances.

About 9 P.M., a unit of around 700 soldiers jogged toward the square from Qian Men, an area directly south of Tiananmen. They were armed with semi-automatic rifles and assault rifles with fixed bayonets. Relatively few people were in the Qian Men area at the time, but when they spotted the troops, 100 ran over, trying to halt the advance. As the people approached, the soldiers raised their rifles and started clubbing their heads. More than 30 were knocked to the ground and the rest dodged out of the way. The troops ran all the way around the square and into the west gate at Zhongnanhai.

Troops were pouring into the city, firing on and killing people everywhere. Often the soldiers laughed wildly. A *Wenhuibao* reporter saw "some troops shooting and laughing at the same time, laughing in a most terrifying manner."

Nearly all witnesses agree that the mass killing of civilians began about 10 P.M., when a convoy of armored personnel carriers rumbled noisily past the apartment complex at Muxidi. People on the street ran for cover without making any attempt to stop them, but troops opened fire anyway. They simply shot at random, and a few people who were not fast enough getting away were shot in the back and died heaped together. The convoy continued east toward Tiananmen, and as they passed the Workers Palace they open up again. This time they not only fired onto both sides of the street, but raised their guns and shot in the direction of people gathered on the rooftops of nearby apartment buildings.

Many residents were standing on the balconies or looking out their windows in a dormitory next to the Workers Palace. The soldiers poured a terrifying volley of automatic weapons fire onto them. An official of the government union who lived on the thirteenth floor was too slow getting out of the way; he took a bullet in the back and fell dead in front of his family. Troops weren't aiming, but scattering bullets across the building.

Pierre Hurel, a correspondent for *Paris Match*, was at a barricade of civilian vehicles west of Muxidi, near the Military History Museum. Crowds were throwing rocks and bottles from the barricade. At 11:30 P.M., a force of 5,000 soldiers led by several hundred sharpshooters broke through the barricade and blasted the crowd with automatic weapons fire. People screamed and ran, and Hurel saw a dozen or more students fall dead. A young man threw a rock and caught a bullet in the chest. The soldier calmly aimed and shot him again.

The same kind of attack happened when soldiers entered the city from the east. As they passed residential areas where townspeople had stopped them earlier, crowds rushed out to prevent them from continuing to Tiananmen. But before the convoy reached the people, the soldiers opened fire. After shooting at them on the street, they raised their guns and fired wildly into the air. A seven-year-old child watching from an apartment roof was hit by one of these stray bullets. An eyewitness wasn't sure if the child died. People were cursing the soldiers, asking what sort of a "people's army" would shoot people just for watching. One cried, "What color hearts do you have anyway?"

Between 9 and 10 P.M. troops suddenly ran toward Tiananmen Square from the west shouting, "Down with the rebellion!" They were stopped and dispersed by the huge crowd on the square. But at that moment a barrage of firing was heard from the southwest, from an area called Xibianmen. People there were trying to stop another troop of fully armed soldiers, who opened fire and fought their way into the city center. An air force helicopter hovered over the square. From 10 P.M. until midnight at least 40 people were killed at Xibianmen.

According to Hua, a convoy of troop trucks was driving toward the square at about 10 P.M. near the Peking Hotel. A woman student from Beijing Normal University stepped up and stopped them. She shouted, "People's Liberation Army men, you're the sons and brothers of the people. We university students are not your enemies; we're your compatriots. We hope you won't turn your rifles on the people. We're not rebels. We're students who love peace and freedom . . ." She was killed in a blaze of gunfire. One of her schoolmates held her body in his arms and wept.

About a quarter after midnight, June 4, two APCs (armored personnel carriers) roared out from Qian Men. They drove as fast as possible, smashing into obstacles in the road and driving directly at any people encountered. One took the road to the east, the other to the west, and they drove north to the Avenue of Eternal Peace. There one turned east and the other west. They roared up and down the avenue several times, one of them even knocking over a truck full of troops and running over a soldier, killing him. When one of these wildly careening APCs came by the grandstands at Tiananmen, the furious crowd threw metal bars between the treads, stopping it. Then they soaked clothing in gasoline and set the vehicle on fire. Two soldiers escaped out of the top of the vehicle and were protected from the crowd's wrath by several students. Many in the crowd were unhappy with the students, Hua said, for saving these soldiers after the army had already killed so many people throughout the city.

Hua and some of his friends in the Public Order Brigades rushed to the Xidan intersection, where a large crowd was trying to stop some advancing tanks. The tanks halted momentarily and people began yelling, "Down with the fascists!" and "Down with tyranny!" At that, machine gunners on the tanks cranked their sights down and opened fire. The entire first row of people fell dying on the street. Then assault troops with the tanks fired and the tanks rolled over the bodies of the dead and wounded.

"I saw it all at the time, the assault rifles, the terrified screaming, then the machine guns—I couldn't completely comprehend what was happening," Hua said. "I ran with my fellow students into the crowd of people at the side of the road. At that moment I heard a burst of machine gun fire. The student on my left stumbled toward the side. I thought he had lost his balance, but when I grabbed his shirt at the chest to pull him up, he was very heavy. Then I looked at his face and I couldn't recognize him. His skull was already splattered open. I put him down instantly. At that point I didn't think of anything; there was no time to think. By that time everybody running beside me had gone down. Three people shot down all at once, including a female student. My fellow students had all disappeared. I just dove for the ground, crawled along the ground, crawled over to where some people were hiding behind a car. The tanks had already rolled by to our left."

Mrs. Li reported that at approximately 1 A.M. two tanks came driving west at high speed toward Tiananmen from the East Avenue of Eternal Peace. They drove back and forth in front of Tiananmen Square wildly driving at anyone who came within their sight. Several people were injured and four people who did not move fast enough were run over and killed at the Jianguo Overpass. The townspeople tried for some time to disable these tanks by throwing various metal objects between the treads. They finally succeeded in stopping one of them in front of the Tiananmen grandstands. Some people then climbed up onto the tank, opened the hatch, and dragged three soldiers out. They beat one of them to death on the spot. One of them was protected by some students and the third one ran safely away from the crowd. The students repeatedly tried to dissuade the crowd from further acts of violence. "We want to maintain our peaceful protest!"

they shouted. By that time the crowd was too angry to listen and they set the disabled tank on fire. Government cameras recorded the incident and used it later as proof that the students "were plotting to overthrow the government" and the rioters "attacked the army."

At 1:30 A.M. beside the History Museum across the street from the square, a reporter for *Wenhuibao* saw a large continent of armed soldiers waiting in the bushes. He started off west down the Avenue of Eternal Peace, and at Zhongshan Park a crowd of screaming people came running east toward Tiananmen, yelling that troops with weapons were coming. Soldiers were chasing them up the avenue, firing as they ran.

Mrs. Li said that at this point, two more tanks came down the Avenue of Eternal Peace from the west. The lead tank sprayed tear gas while the rear tank opened fire with machine guns, shooting as it went down the street. It killed many people.

Hua said that sometime before 2:30 A.M. at the History Museum, he saw a woman student bayoneted in the chest as she confronted the soldiers. She fell to the ground and a soldier ran up and stabbed her several more times until she died. As the students ran away from these troops, they were cut down from behind by automatic weapons fire. Then the tanks ran right over them. About twenty women students were killed that way at the same time.

"They were all run over," he said. "If they weren't run over, they were raked by machine gun fire. If they didn't die, they were given a second and a third shot. Not to leave any living witnesses." This slaughter went on for hours all around the perimeter of Tiananmen Square.

According to Mrs. Li, people on the square were extremely agitated after the tank attack. She heard Chai Ling, the woman who was the general commander of the Students Autonomous Association, announce over the loudspeakers, "Fellow students, please remain calm! Students who want to withdraw can do so now. Those who don't want to leave can remain here with me!" Then a large force of armed police came into the avenue and drove Mrs. Li and many others away.

The sky over the Avenue of Eternal Peace was lit by a hail of tracer bullets about 2:15 A.M. The area of the avenue that forms the northern boundary of Tiananmen Square was occupied by troops, who moved the people to the east and cleared an open space. Troops now ranged on all four sides of the square.

From 3 to 4 A.M., APCs and tanks poured in from the west while soldiers grouped west of the square in front of the Great Hall of the

People. Another unit formed up at Qian Men and shouted at the crowds to disperse, and later chased people away with gunfire.

Mrs. Li heard the sound of shooting coming from the square at 2:30. A large crowd formed around the area and faced off with troops who were about 100 yards away on the avenue. She said it was the 27th Army, and that they had surrounded the square. They refused to allow ambulances in to pick up the wounded, and she saw a paramedic shot dead by the army.

"A city bus driver drove his bus onto the square, jumped down and risked his life to load on the wounded and drive them to the hospital," she said. "After a few trips he was cut down, but his place was immediately taken by another person. When this bullet-riddled vehicle made its last trip to the hospital, breaking down completely, the driver collapsed and never got up again; it was the fifth driver."

A man covered with blood told her, "Don't be afraid. This is other people's blood. Watching them slaughter people like that, I really didn't feel like living! Listen to me and don't forget it, I've personally picked up 173 people and more than ten of them died in my arms. You remember that, you!"

After watching the slaughter on the avenue for an hour or so, Mrs. Li ran away to the Nan Chizi area and sat down someplace in a daze.

Hua returned to the square between 2:30 and 3:30 A.M. in a state of shock. Sitting beside the Monument to the Revolutionary Martyrs with his friends and fellow students, they all resolved to die for the cause. He said everybody was calm and silent, sitting there "with but one thought – death."

He had argued before that the most beautiful conclusion to the movement would be a massacre. "I didn't think there could be any better ending. Everyone was prepared to die. We even shouted out around the square, 'Fellow students, don't panic. We have sworn to defend Tiananmen Square to the death! The time has come to protect our nation's honor with our blood! The time has come to protect democracy.'"

Hou Dejian, the former Taiwan singer who had joined the hunger strike at the last minute, said things weren't nearly so calm on the square. (He wrote a report on the massacre from the Australian Embassy on June 12, which was published in the *World Journal*.) Everyone was extremely frightened but they were making heroic efforts to appear calm, he wrote. Two older companions, Zhou Tuo of the Stone Computer Corporation and the journalist Gao Xin, suggested they should try to get the students to leave while there was still time. But Hou and the other penitential hunger stiker – Liu Xiaopo, the young lecturer – didn't agree.

Then they heard Chai Ling's announcement about students leaving if they wished. They were afraid her statement would destroy the unity and discipline of the people on the square. If some began to panic and run away, they thought, the army would open fire. They decided to try and evacuate the students.

They persuaded student leaders to go along with a withdrawal – all but Chai Ling. She said she believed if they held the square until daybreak, high officials would be able to control the army. Apparently she had heard this from sources she trusted. The other four didn't agree with her. They persuaded several workers who had captured weapons to give them up – a machine gun, two semi-automatic rifles and a pistol. The weapons were destroyed while reporters took pictures.

According to Hua, Hou then got on the loudspeaker and appealed to the army. "Martial law officers and soldiers, I'm Hou Dejian. On behalf of our four-man hunger strike group, I want to ask you to negotiate with us for a minute, to find a way to let the students leave the square safely." The army didn't send anyone over to negotiate.

Hou wrote that at 3:30 A.M. he talked to two Red Cross doctors, who suggested they take an ambulance over to negotiate with the army commanders. Hou, Zhou, the doctors and several members of the Public Order Brigades drove over to find the troop leaders. Near the square's northeast corner, stretching along the Avenue of Eternal Peace, there were more than 10,000 assault troops. They stopped the car, got out, and ran toward the soldiers. With a loud "clack clack clack" many soldiers slipped rounds into the firing chambers of their weapons. They immediately halted and one of the doctors identified Hou to the troops, saying he wanted to talk with their commander.

They negotiated with a three-star general named Ji who said he was a Political Commissar and that he had to clear their request with higher authorities. While the general was gone, the lights went out and the soldiers became extremely agitated, cocking their guns, yelling wildly and stamping on the broken glass that littered the ground. The general came back and said the safest way to evacuate would be to go toward the southeast.

All reports I've come across say the lights went out at about 4 A.M. According to *Wenhuibao*, government loudspeakers then announced that the "disturbance" had become a "counter-revolutionary rebellion."

Thousands of people were on the east side and south end of the square, in front of the History Museum, Mao's Tomb, and the Monument to the Revolutionary Martyrs. An estimated 5,000 to 10,000 people, mostly students, but some workers, were on Tiananmen Square itself. Many were sitting on the three levels leading up to the base of the monument and on its base, singing "The International" as troops closed in.

Hua said Hou Dejian then told those at the monument, "Fellow students, I hope that you will forgive me for doing something imprudent, but now I ask you in my own name to please leave the square. Fellow students, we've lost enough blood already. You shouldn't have the slightest illusion about this kind of a party and this kind of a government. What we're waiting for now is a bloody massacre. We've got to save our strength for the future. Don't wait any longer. Fellow students, I'm certain that not one of you remaining here is afraid of dying."

Several yelled at him after each sentence, such things as, "Hou Dejian, you get the hell out of here, you coward! Don't give us all that crap! If you want to leave, you go ahead and leave!"

But now there was increasingly loud gunfire from the west side of the monument. Hua said he heard the soldiers' crazed laughter as they fired.

Then two of the other hunger strikers, Zhou Tuo and Liu Xiaopo, took over and repeatedly urged the students to leave. Hou wrote that people were starting to change their minds about staying to the end.

The shooting was getting closer. Hou noticed troops moving in from the direction of Qian Men in the south. He was afraid this would cause a panic so he decided once more to ask General Ji to give them more time to evacuate. He ran to the northeast, where he found Ji leading his troops in. The general told him the time was up and he had to complete his mission. He advised Hou and his friends to leave on their own if they couldn't persuade the students to evacuate.

"The four of us are staying to the end. If we were afraid of death, we would have left long ago," Hou said. A soldier at the general's side pointed his weapon at them and yelled.

Hou and the rest ran as fast as they could back to the monument, shouting all the way, "Hurry up and leave! Go to the southeast!"

As students filed out slowly, Hua recalled, the police pursued them, firing into the ground and beating them on the back with clubs. The army also chased them with rifles and bayonets. Many women students were beaten bloody, lost their shoes, had their clothes nearly ripped off. Others stumbled and fell, and were trampled to death.

Another barrage of tracer bullets flew into the black sky at 4:40 A.M., and at this signal the lights came on again, bright as day.

CHAPTER 8

UNDER THE GATE OF HELL

SOLDIERS STORMED OUT OF THE GREAT HALL OF THE People. Wearing helmets, fatigues and gas masks, and carrying assault rifles, they charged to a point directly west of the Monument to the Revolutionary Martyrs and quickly set up a row of machine guns. (This report was given by a student from Qing Hua University, who spoke with Hong Kong's *Wenhuibao*. Other witnesses had similar accounts.)

A second wave of soldiers and military police with plastic clubs and electric prods formed up directly to the north of the monument. They beat and pushed their way through the students until they had cleared a path to the top of the monument's base. Just as the troops were pushing in from the north, another group of soldiers carrying rifles charged in from the east. Once there, they started firing their rifles in the air and shoving students off the monument.

Hou Dejian and Chai Ling saw troops shoot up the student loudspeakers on the monument. Some troops recognized the singer and yelled, "Hou Dejian, hurry up, get out of here!" Many students to the north of the monument had refused to move. He rushed to them, pleading with them to leave, saying there was no point in dying that way. Just as they began to follow him, riot police pounced on them, clubbing them. Rows of people were knocked to the ground. Hou was injured, but rescued by a Public Order Brigade member who pulled him out of the way.

His friend Liu Xiaopo, the young university lecturer, then hurried back and helped the two others to reach a Red Cross aid station on the west side of the History Museum. Hou collapsed on a stretcher and rested there for an hour and a half.

While this was going on, two groups of armored personnel carriers moved in simultaneously. One formed a near-circle around the monument, leaving only an opening near the History Museum to the northeast, and kept tightening the loop. The other group formed a column four abreast and several vehicles long, and drove directly at the protesters around the monument. They gradually forced them away from the monument to the south. The students and townspeople linked arms and retreated in the face of the oncoming vehicles.

At that, the army opened fire all over the square and the sky was filled with tracers again—as if the army wanted people to believe they were only firing into the air. But the machine guns in front of the monument were actually firing straight ahead into the crowd. Soldiers and military police on the monument's top level beat, shoved and bayoneted the students, pushing them to the ground level. As soon as they were off the monument, machine guns raked them. The survivors surged back on, looking for cover, but the troops beat them back and the machine guns opened up again. At the same time the APCs pushed closer to the students as they fired their machine guns, even knocking over the flagpoles around the monument.

Some of the people tried to break out of the encirclement toward the east. Under ceaseless fire from machine guns and automatic rifles, A Dare to Die Brigade managed to push an APC over on its side, thus clearing a path out. They ran for safety in four waves. In the first wave a survivor estimated 3,000 students dashed over to the steps of the History Museum, but only about 1,000 made it. The last wave broke out sometime after 5 A.M.

The escapees joined with townspeople who had been there all along, and retreated north toward the Avenue of Eternal Peace. Before they could move very far, they came under fire from troops lying in ambush there. Then they turned around and ran south toward Qian Men.

Hua claimed that while all this was going on, exhausted students still slept in some of the more than 100 small tents on the square. It's hard to believe anyone could sleep through that noise, but a student from the Beijing Institute of Chemical Engineering said he kicked a sleeping friend of his to arouse him just before he ran off the square. He wasn't certain if anyone else was in the tents, and his friend turned up at school the next day.

Hua said that for several nights, students had been so worried about being attacked they didn't sleep. He was certain that some of the tents were occupied at the time of the attack.

"When I returned from outside to the monument, I saw many students sleeping all around, some on the ground, some on cots donated by Beijing townspeople, and some in the tents. There were so many students; just as we started to move off—we didn't have time to wake up these sleeping students—ten or more tanks rolled right over their bodies. Ten or more tanks in a line rolled right over all of the tents crushing them into little pieces. APCs also rolled right over all of them. If we had moved off only two minutes later, when the APCs came rolling up we'd have been crushed to death for sure."

Hua encountered the people fleeing south toward Qian Men from the History Museum. Somewhere near the museum he saw a woman student from Beijing Normal University lying on the ground without shoes, her clothing was in shreds. He picked her up and carried her to the east, as shots continued to ring out behind them. When they reached Dongjiao Minxiang, a street south of the Beijing Hotel, some people saw him struggling to carry the young woman while soldiers were chasing them.

People began to shout at the slowly approaching tanks, "Down with fascism! Down with the beasts! You're all a gang of thugs!" The tanks immediately fired on the crowd and a squad of soldiers rushed at them, shooting their assault rifles. Hua hit the ground with his arms around the wounded coed and crawled along dragging her with him.

"I couldn't carry her because I'd have been shot," he said. By some stroke of luck they finally got away. Later that day he encountered several more angry citizens who told him how the troops had fired on them around 10 A.M., June 4, near the police station on the Avenue of Eternal Peace, killing the fiancee of a young man who was wounded himself.

While Mrs. Li was sitting dazed by what she had seen, she met a man who looked even more beat-up than she did. He said he was one of the few survivors of the massacre and told her that when the lights went out at 4 A.M., there were many people on the square trying to rescue the wounded. When the lights went on again at 4:40 he could see bodies all over the place.

The army wouldn't allow anyone to carry off the wounded, and soldiers came around administering a *coup de grace* to anyone wounded. A young woman tried to get up after she was shot in the shoulder. Before she could stand, a soldier ran over, plunged his bayonet into her chest and ripped her open from top to bottom. The man who told of this was so frightened that his legs gave out. He slumped to the ground and began to crawl away. As he was inching away from the middle of the square, he heard the rumble of a convoy of at least 100 tanks pulling up. From a distance he saw the tanks line up like harvesters and roll over everything in the square, including all the tents, in which he also believed people were still sleeping. "For the sake of history," he said, he looked at his watch. It took the tanks exactly seven minutes to roll across everything in the square.

By this time, the army had launched a full-scale attack on the entire area surrounding Tiananmen Square. At 4:30 A.M., 30 tanks and a large number of troop trucks and supply trucks rolled up the West Avenue of Eternal Peace, going from Muxidi to the square.

About 5 A.M., another convoy of six tanks and ten or more trucks roared toward the square from the east firing automatic weapons indiscriminately all the way along the East Avenue of Eternal Peace.

Also about this time, a club-wielding unit attacked people around Zhushikou, a district several blocks south of Qian Men. People began to fight back. Sporadic fighting continued in that area all day and night and into June 5.

Shortly before 5 A.M. June 4, several people saw three tanks chase a group of students west on the West Avenue. The students had just escaped from the square and were trying to retreat in the direction of the university quarter toward the northwest. The tanks sped up behind them and ran over at least ten.

I recorded a Peking University student's report of this incident at 10 A.M. in the Free Speech Triangle. He had started on his bike from the Minzu Hotel going toward the square to look for bodies of his classmates. Near Xidan he met people who were running west away from the square. They told him that when the tanks had arrived, Hou Dejian came out to negotiate with the troops and an agreement was reached in which the students would leave and the troops wouldn't fire on them.

As the students were trooping off the square, some of them shouted slogans. At that, the army opened fire and the tanks moved in. They saw the tanks run over "a group of eleven students" from behind.

Ignoring their warnings that it wasn't safe, this man said he had to go and see if any of the dead were from Beida. A mile or so down the avenue at Liubukou, he came upon a row of bodies ground into pulp, crushed into their bicycles. It was impossible to identify them. He saw tanks coming, thought they were going to run over the bodies a second time, and got on his bike and hurried away. Later in the morning he saw a photograph of the same pile of bodies posted outside of the People's University, where some of the dead students evidently were from.

Students from outside Beijing were hiding in an underground walkway. They had run in there thinking it would be safe from the tanks and APCs. A student from the Beijing Institute of Chemical

Engineering who escaped from the square told a reporter from the Hong Kong magazine *Bai Xing* that the army fired machine guns into both ends of an underground walkway. "All of the out-of-town students died in there," he said.

He too saw tanks and APCs chasing students off the square. "Eleven students from Qing Hua University ran too slowly and were ran over," he said. Also, "after these soldiers killed some people they would raise their rifles in the air, laugh, and shout about their victory."

By 5:40 A.M., an hour after the carnage began, the army had control of Tiananmen Square. Rows of tanks, APCs and armed soldiers lined up all over the square. In another hour, heavy clouds of smoke rose over the square as the army set about burning everything left behind. An eyewitness told Mrs. Li that he went to the square about 7 A.M.

"I saw the tanks and the military vehicles lined up on the square," he said. "Altogether there were five large bonfires. The flames were about 30 feet high and black smoke rose straight into the air. I also saw some soldiers pouring alcohol onto the flames . . . burning the corpses this way to hide the evidence."

He told Mrs. Li that when the history of the terrible event is written, "it'll be very difficult to tell exactly how many people were killed. There were so many out-of-town students and we don't even know their names."

People living near the Beijing Hotel smelled alcohol and a terrible stench they believed was burning bodies.

Other witnesses told Hong Kong reporters that earth movers hauled away the ashes and a sanitation unit sprayed the area with disinfectant; that soldiers put corpses in plastic bags and piled them on trucks and helicopters to be hauled off; that crumpled bodies lay in heaps all over the square, and soldiers covered them with canvas; that troops piled up bodies and burned them on the square.

Cheng Ying of the Hong Kong publication *The Ninties* wrote that on June 4, the Beijing crematorium workers refused to burn any bodies until they were positively identified. So the army took over and troops began cremating unidentified victims.

After dawn, crowds gathered around to see what was happening on the square. Troops stationed at Mao's Mausoleum south of the monument fired a barrage of tear gas, then attacked with clubs to disperse them.

One professor's son, who was a student, failed to returned from Tiananmen on June 4. The family assumed he was dead but they were determined to locate his body at any cost. They searched for hours through Beijing's overcrowded morgues. When they finally found his bullet-riddled body, he was wearing a complete army uniform. He was only a student—what was he doing in a uniform? His family thinks the army must have dressed some civilian casualties in uniform in order to photograph them and claim them as soldiers killed by "counter-revolutionary rebels."

Troops entering Beijing throughout the morning of June 4 continued to open fire, killing group after group of civilians.

Mrs. Li went onto the streets again at 9 A.M. At Nan Chizi she watched in horror as a crowd of unarmed people squared off against a troop formation about 100 yards away on the Avenue of Eternal Peace. The people would shout such things as, "We're not rebels; you've been tricked by propaganda!" and "Don't be fooled by those evil men; don't kill your own compatriots!" In every case, the army's response was gunfire, and every time they shot a few more people fell dead or wounded.

Scenes such as this were witnessed from the windows and rooftops of the Beijing Hotel by reporters like Pierre Hurel, and were videotaped by news crews from around the world.

Troops across the avenue in front of Tiananmen fired volleys into the crowd only 100 yards away. They used assault rifles and even pistols. The crowd would run for cover and several would be left dead or wounded in the street, and some brave people would rush out to drag a few of the wounded off.

The soldiers followed their victims to the hospitals. A nurse in a Beijing hospital, who is now living abroad, told a Chinese friend of mine that after many horribly wounded people were brought to the hospital, troops showed up too. Officers ordered the doctors and nurses to stay away from the wounded. If they refused to stop treating them, they would be shot or beaten. Young nurses stood on the other side of the room or hall from the wounded, crying as the victims writhed in pain and slowly bled to death. The nurses begged to let them attend to the wounded, but the officers were remorseless.

After he escaped to Paris, a high-ranking party official named Yan Zhun said police and army units locked several hundred dead and wounded people in the basement of the Palace Museum behind Tiananmen, leaving them for several hours without medical attention. Many of the wounded died, and the troops brought their corpses to the Public Security Hospital.

The Peking University student who had gone in search of dead students witnessed another battle as he was riding west on the Avenue of Eternal Peace, after he saw the crushed bodies. A row of APCs had been halted by a large crowd, who began to set fire to them. The soldiers stayed inside until they were engulfed in flames. They were damned scared, he said, and when they finally climbed out of the vehicles, their T-shirts were soaked with sweat. When they hit the ground, the furious people rushed over to attack them. Several students yelled for them to run in their direction, so they ran between the APCs to the students.

The students ordered them to drop their weapons and take off their uniforms, and they did. Then the students began to lecture them about the Democracy Movement. The soldiers said they were from Shanxi Province, they knew nothing of the situation in Beijing, and their officers told them in a meeting just a couple of days ago that they would never fire on the students.

The Beida student commented here that no one could believe that, and that the troops who had killed the students on the square had banners on their vehicles reading, "The People's Liberation Army loves the people!"

These soldiers said the killers were from the 27th Army from Shijiazhuang in Hebei Province, and they showed the crowd they didn't have live ammunition in their weapons. This was in spite of the fact that shooting had been going on elsewhere for several hours.

As he left, one of the townspeople said more than 130 APCs had been set afire. Another put the number at 85, and said it happened on the avenue near the Military Museum. The student himself saw at least 30 APCs torched.

Chinese newspapers said some soldiers shed their uniforms and went into hiding. The government itself has said 1,000 rifles are missing.

The wounded singer, Hou Dejian, reached Capital Hospital at 8 A.M. A friend, with the pseudonym Xiao Zhang, a Beijing Normal University student who was with him on the square, visited him secretly at the hospital. Hou told him, "I was only stabbed a couple of times with a bayonet. I'm all right. Go see about the others in the hall."

Xiao Zhang talked with a friend who worked at the hospital. The friend said some army officers wouldn't allow ambulances to remove the wounded from Tiananmen Square, but that this man saved some by covering them with sheets and pretending they were dead. By the time they reached the hospital, some of them had in fact expired.

While they were talking, Zhang heard a big commotion outside. He walked out and saw two unarmed soldiers, one of them jumping around wildly and literally frothing at the mouth. Zhang's friend said, "They were brought in by the Martial Law Forces. One of them has already lost his mind and the other is about to crack up too."

Xiao Zhang grabbed the soldier who was jumping and asked, "What did you do?"

"I ran over and killed a lot of girl students. Ha, ha, I completed my mission. I want to go home to Mama!"

The other soldier, who was more rational, said, "Our company commander saw the students lined up in front of our armored personnel carrier and reported to the regimental commander that we could not go on. Suddenly the regimental commander walked up, pulled out his pistol and shot the company commander dead. Then he forced us to drive over the students. The students, they wouldn't move out of the way and we crushed quite a few of them. He went off his head immediately; I fainted and was sent to the hospital. All we ask is for the doctor to give us a couple of proof-of-insanity forms and then we'll leave."

He said quite a few recruits went crazy from killing. Some of them were killed – it wasn't clear by whom – and others were sent to the hospital.

Doctors at the Capital Hospital said they were too busy with the wounded and dying to treat these two shell-shocked soldiers, so they just let them stew in the courtyard.

A Beijing newsman told a *Bai Xing* reporter another story about dissension in the ranks. He was helping a wounded youth when they ran into a large crowd near the Dongzhimen Overpass, three or four miles north from Tiananmen. Many troops were under the overpass. When he showed the crowd and the troops that the young man's wounds obviously were inflicted by army bullets, two platoon leaders grew agitated. They withdrew momentarily from the group, then came striding back, cocked their automatic rifles, and shot and killed the major who commanded their battalion. They were shouting that he had tricked them, told them they were in Beijing to take some outdoor pictures, he was "too ruthless." The people gathered around these two, protecting them and helping them run away.

The random slaughter continued in Beijing for two or three days, until the city was beaten into submission. Soldiers were indeed attacked by angry crowds with rocks and fire bombs. The people of Beijing sought revenge for friends and family members gunned down on June 3 and 4. Eventually they had to surrender to an iron-fisted army of occupation. But it is a sullen submission, and it may not be permanent.

The student Hua kept the hope alive that there would be another confrontation. He ended his eyewitness report to other students by saying, "I hope all the living, all those who did not experience this bloody scene—I hope other people do not die like our fellow students.

"I hope the living can do something to make the deaths of our fellow students more worthwhile. Their deaths are very valuable. And I hope everyone will take some action to make their deaths even more worthwhile. Everyone should use whatever little strength he has. If you remain silent, then the deaths of our fellow students on Tiananmen Square will have been for nothing.

"Although I didn't die, I feel terribly bad. I feel like the others died in my place. I should have died. I will still die later. This regime has already gone this far, they can eliminate anyone who knows the true story. I know everything that happened because I escaped off of Tiananmen Square. I hope such a situation will arise again in the future. I hope that I will be able to die because I want to use my own blood to awaken even more people. . . .

"Finally, I beg you, in your happiest moments please pray for all of our fellow students who died on the square! Let them rest a little easier in heaven."

The above eyewitness reports demonstrate an undeniable fact: the Tiananmen Massacre was a deliberately planned and executed slaughter of unarmed citizens by a political regime that considered them its enemies. There are thousands of surviving eyewitnesses; less than a hundred have been able to make their stories public. Although their accounts differ in many particulars of time and place, they are in general agreement as to the main facts.

CHAPTER 9

MOURNING FOR CHINA

I WOKE ON SUNDAY, JUNE 4, JUST IN TIME TO HEAR THE VOICE of America's English language report of hundreds killed in Beijing when troops fired on crowds, with bodies strewn all over Tiananmen Square. Chinese TV carried no pictures of the massacre, but talked about a "counter-revolutionary rebellion" for the first time. I needed to get my bike fixed and see what I could find out.

I walked my bike through sad crowds on campus. Everyone was wearing black armbands. Mournful music was playing on the loudspeakers. As I arrived at the university post office, a flatbed truck pulled up with students in the back, one stretching a bloody T-shirt in his hands, holding it over his head. He shouted angrily to the crowd, telling of the slaughter, concluding, "A debt of blood must be repaid in blood!" His white headband had the same words, written in black ink. I went into a campus store, bought a strip of black cloth for 50 cents, and tied it onto my left arm.

A banner strung between two trees just inside the school's South Gate read *Can jue renhuan*, "Tragic beyond human imagination." While my bike was being repaired by a sullen, uncommunicative old man at the bicycle shop, which was just beyond the South Gate, I joined a crowd gathered around a street sign on the corner. Pushing my way to the front, I saw four Polaroid photographs had been pasted up: a pile of crumpled young bodies with their heads shot full of holes, blood dripping, lying upon the mangled steel bars of their bicycles; several clumps of bodies riddled with bullet holes lying on the sidewalks and in the streets.

After my bicycle was repaired, I rode a couple of blocks south on Baishiqiao Road. People were pedaling along the street as usual, but a large group was gathered around a utility pole to read a hand-lettered leaflet. Several people helped me read the cursive characters. The sign told the story of the massacre from an eyewitness point of view.

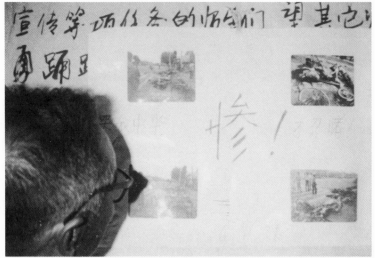

"Tragic! I weep for my China! Too horrible to look at!"

Tanks, armored cars and troop trucks broke through the lines of people at Muxidi in the middle of the night and began crushing and shooting people indiscriminately as they made their way east toward Tiananmen, the poster said. Old men, old women and small children were shot dead. People were even shot and wounded inside their apartments. Tanks crushed people in the streets. The author continually referred to the troops as fascists and beasts and said they were "without any vestige of humanity."

As I was reading this, a loud noise, like an explosion, came from a few blocks down the road. I rode over to take a look, and saw two vehicles on fire at the large traffic circle. Heading back to Beida, I stopped to read another leaflet pasted on a traffic sign. It gave a detailed report of the number of dead and wounded admitted to six Beijing hospitals as of 6 A.M.—about 200 altogether.

Several more photos of the carnage had been stuck on the wall to the right of Beida's South Gate. I moved close and snapped a picture. Their caption read, "Tragic! I weep for my China! Too horrible to look at!" One of the pictures was eventually printed in Hong Kong newspapers, then photocopied from the paper and posted all over Beijing in the next couple of days.

A couplet to the right and left of the gate read, "It is not that the people have no government, but the government has no people."

118

An eyewitness report began on the loudspeaker. This was the talk by the Peking University student who had searched for dead students, had seen bodies crushed by tanks and watched a crowd fire a row of APCs.

He began by saying he was taking an oath on his life that everything he reported he saw with his own eyes. He was on the steps of the Minzu Hotel last night and this morning. Police and troops in armored cars attacked unarmed civilians without any provocation on the street in front of the hotel. People fell and died there in front of his eyes and bullets flew over his head before he and several others rushed into the hotel lobby for safety.

Toward the end of his 30-minute talk, he said he witnessed the carnage in several hospitals. That morning at the Post and Telecommunications Hospital, bodies were lying all around in the hallways. Exhausted doctors and nurses had been operating all night. By the time he got there they had no more anesthetics and no proper sterilization. The floors were covered with blood and the stench was terrible. The dead students and workers had their faces beaten beyond recognition, or blown apart by dumdum or armor-piercing bullets that left gaping holes. He saw people with bowels blasted open or with lips, teeth, jaws and eyes shot away. He read a list of some of the dead that he saw, most of which were on the third floor:

—Fuerke, male 19 years old, Nationalities University, class of '88.

—Wu Guohui, male, 19 years old, People's University, Industrial Economics, class of '86, student number 6070115. His entire face was painted white. He asked the nurse the reason for this and she said his face was destroyed by the bullet and this was all they could do for the body's appearance.

—Du Lijun, female, Beijing Normal University, Education Department, class of '86.

—Liu Zhong, male, 19 years of age, from Shanghai, University of Government and Law, Political Science.

—Duan Changlong, male, Qing Hua University, Chemical Engineering.

—No identification found, male, wearing Beijing Normal University badge.

—No name found, female, also from Beijing Normal. Dead on arrival, bowels shot completely out of her body.

—No name, male, Beijing Agricultural Institute, Agricultural Economics Department. Alive on arrival, he was carried out of the emergency room door dead five minutes later.

–Ten males and one female without identification papers of any kind.

–Xu Ruihe, a young man who recently was released from the army.

–Ma Senyou, 27, who worked for the Ministry of Industry and Commerce.

–Ma Junfei, a little boy, the son of the above victim.

By 5:15 A.M. in this single hospital, there were already 28 corpses, most of them students. He did not give any particulars on eight.

He watched an operation in which a doctor removed a two-inch bullet from a student's back. The student weighed the bullet in his palm and told the doctor he would keep it the rest of his life.

A young man who was not a student was sitting, waiting, and kept asking, "When are you going to take care of me? It's only a small wound." Then he pulled back his shirt sleeve, and showed a gaping hole through his upper arm.

"That's what passed for a minor wound," the witness commented.

Another man, a student, had a wound the size of a dime. It would not stop bleeding. A doctor was trying to staunch the flow with his bare hands while the young man yelled and writhed in pain and his girlfriend wept at his side.

When the Peking University student finished, he again swore on his life that he had seen it all with his own eyes. He angrily said all this killing was ordered by Emperor Deng Xiaoping because he was going to die soon and "he wants to take a few thousand people with him to wait on him in hell!"

The Student Broadcast Station continued to announce the names and departments of dead students for an hour or so. An announcement from the Peking University Students Autonomous Association urged students not to make any more unnecessary sacrifices. It was time to prepare memorial services to honor their fallen comrades, it said. The announcement outlined efforts to inform the entire country of what had happened, and said the association intended to call for a general strike and continue the nonviolent struggle for democracy. At least 2,100 were dead, the association believed.

I went back to my room. At about 11 A.M., Edward Gargan, the journalist, showed up with a fellow reporter. "They slaughtered those students. They really slaughtered them," Gargan said. He sank into a chair, took off his sunglasses, and wiped his eyes. He'd been on the square last night, felt bullets flying over his head, and thought he was going to be killed.

"That was the first time in my life anybody was shooting at me!" he said. "I thought I was going to die right there."

While I was telling him about the reports on the loudspeakers, the phone rang. It was a professional man, a friend of mine, who wanted to tell me the truth about some of the things I would soon see on CCTV. He said the story was true about a soldier being hung from Fuxing Gate, doused with gasoline and set on fire. The soldier had just shot and killed several unarmed civilians including a little girl and an elderly couple, he said. When he ran out of ammunition, the angry crowd grabbed him. He deserved it. My friend said he knew about this incident from an acquaintance who saw it all. By calling me, he risked arrest because my telephone almost certainly was tapped.

"You have to tell the outside world!" he said. He also said many more were killed than had been reported. He was sure from what other people saw that the army had burned many corpses.

After Gargan left, I sat for a long time like a zombie. The enormity of what had happened last night was beginning to sink in. For the first time since I came to Beijing I just stayed in my room and listened to the radio in the daytime.

Chinese Central Radio claimed a "counter-revolutionary rebellion" had been victoriously put down, and threatened punishment for anyone who continued to resist. Then BBC's 4 P.M. broadcast repeated the true story for the world to hear. One incident reported by the BBC was that a Chinese broadcaster on an English language program had blurted out, "My government just killed thousands of innocent people." The word going around Beijing was that this man, named Li Dan, director of the English Section of Beijing International Broadcasting Station, was immediately taken out and shot.

According to a Hong Kong journal, the morning of the massacre Li said, "This is the Beijing International Broadcasting Station. Please remember that on June 3, 1989, there occurred in China's capital, Beijing, a frightening tragedy. Thousands of people, most of them innocent civilians, were killed by armed soldiers who forced their way into the city. Some of our own International Broadcasting Station employees were also among the casualties."

He went on to describe the massacre, and his broadcast was picked up and taped by the BBC. The Hong Kong reporters heard the BBC broadcast, translated it into Chinese, and I retranslated it into English from the journal. The paper called Li contemporary China's "most courageous journalist."

Several reporters and other workers at CCTV, *People's Daily*,

Guangming Daily and other media were arrested on charges of aiding the "rebellion." The editor of *People's Daily* was fired and replaced by an army officer. Rumors said Wei Hua, a CCTV anchorwoman who had recently told an American television network that Deng Xiaoping should retire, was either shot or arrested. These rumors apparently were unfounded. Wei Hua is now said to have been unharmed.

Professor Yang Xianyi, a famous translator and editor for Panda Books, was interviewed by the BBC. It was a courageous act for him. He called the massacre "the most shameful thing the Chinese government has ever done," and said the killer troops were the private army of Chairman Deng Xiaoping and President Yang Shangkun. He accused Deng and Yang of being "the greatest criminals in Chinese history." He was an old man, he said, and they could kill him if they wished, but "China has one billion people and they cannot kill us all."

Listening to his voice, I was very touched. I recalled his frail, slim, white-headed figure, his love of Chinese literature, his zest for life, and his support for young Chinese writers and artists. I especially remember the warmth with which he and his wife Gladys received my wife and me into their home in the spring of 1987. Yang also gave a videotape interview for American television at his home after the massacre. The overseas Chinese press reported in October that the Yangs had been visited by Ying Ruocheng, the Vice Minister of Culture. This may be seen as an attempt to demonstrate the current regime's leniency. But an American friend who lived in Beijing last year told me Yang was forced to make a strong self-criticism in order to escape punishment.

I stayed in my room in Shaoyuan all afternoon, listening to the radio, reading Democracy Movement pamphlets, numb from what I had seen and heard. I reflected on what had happened. For a week or more, this was a completely orderly society, city life was normal, there was absolutely no "disturbance," only a peaceful protest in the square. Orders were given not just to clear the Square—that could have been done with much less loss of life—but to kill many people on purpose to frighten away the rest. Those who ordered this slaughter—Deng, Yang, Li and the rest—will never allow China to become a democratic political entity, because that would mean the end of their dictatorial powers and that of their children. It seemed to me that only a long, nonviolent resistance could bring the government down, and then only if a great number of workers participated in it. If not, China would become worse than Czechoslovakia after the repression of the Prague Spring in 1968.

At seven o'clock I turned on the CCTV news as usual wondering how the hell they would treat the massacre. I shall never forget the words on the screen that evening. The screen came up in dark blue with no pictures (they had not yet pasted together their phony videos), only the following Big Lie in white letters: *Xuexi Tiananmen Guangchang shu yaoyan,* "Bloodbath on Tiananmen Square is a false rumor." The voice behind the words read it out several times and then went on to say "rumor-mongers" were spreading the false story of a bloodbath on Tiananmen Square. What really happened, said this faceless voice, was that a mob of "ruffians," "hooligans," and "rioters" had mounted a "counter-revolutionary rebellion" trying to overthrow the government and it had been put down in a "great victory" by the People's Liberation Army. The students had all left the square peacefully without anyone even being hurt. The People's Liberation Army never fired on or killed any civilians.

As George Orwell said in *1984,* "he who controls the past controls the future." The Chinese Communist Party Central Propaganda Department always operates on this principle. This whole lying story was soon to become the everyday propaganda line of the new leadership. The lies went on and on for several minutes as the television news became radio news because they could not show any pictures of something that did not actually happen.

After watching this, I had to get out of that little room. I rode to the Student Broadcast Station. The loudspeakers were playing plaintive music alternating with speeches about their dead comrades and the need to carry on the struggle for democracy. Large black characters several feet high had been painted over the rows of big character posters: "Repay a debt of blood with blood!" and "Hang the executioner Li Peng!" and "An inhuman atrocity!"

On the loudspeakers, the Peking University Student Leadership Group was calling on students to remember that the most important things now were to bury their dead with the proper mourning rites, to prepare to carry on the nonviolent struggle, and not to make any further unnecessary sacrifices.

Everyone was waiting for the army to take over the university, and the leaders didn't want any more senseless killing. "They are bound to come," a middle-aged professor told me. "The question is when."

I biked slowly around Beida's Weiming Lake, with its picture-postcard water tower in the style of an ancient pagoda. I thought of my wife back in Vancouver and of the many pleasant afternoon walks we made around this artificial lake in 1986–87. I recalled one afternoon when we talked to a group of school children on their way home. They were trying to catch insects, but when they caught one they set it free. I asked why they were freeing the bugs. A charming little boy beamed up at us and said in his crisp Beijing dialect, "Look! It's a dragonfly. A good insect, very beautiful." Very beautiful. And so was he, and so were the hopes for democracy and justice of the students, workers, and people of Beijing.

Mournful music continued to weep through the gradually darkening air.

CHAPTER 10

ESCAPE FROM BEIJING

S TREET FIGHTING WAS GOING ON IN BEIJING, ACCORDING
to the Voice of America news on Monday morning, June
5. Thousands of citizens were battling the soldiers, and
some were armed with weapons given to them by People's
Liberation Army troops. Chinese Central Radio called
Sunday's carnage a suppression of counter- revolutionaries who wanted
to use the National People's Congress to set up a "people's government." That was a rare slip, admitting that the present regime was not
a people's government.

Allan Pessin reported on the 8 A.M. Voice of America "Newsline"
that at least 1,400 people were believed killed Sunday. Tanks and APCs
were still being attacked with fire-bombs. The Great Hall of the People
was surrounded by the army and troops were said to be burning piles
of corpses to prevent an accurate count of the dead.

At the Free Speech Triangle the Chinese National Anthem and
"The International" were broadcast alternately, sounding like a dirge.
People were standing around talking about the massacre, listening to
short reports, reading posters. Sadness and angry resignation were
etched in their faces. A crowd immediately formed around me, asking
what the American people think about what was happening and what
the American government would do. I told them those American
people who want to know do know what has happened in China; they
will support the students because most of the American people are
basically in favor of freedom and democracy everywhere in the world.
The American government was another matter, I added: President Bush
had already condemned the troops' violence, but had done nothing
else so far.

"The Communist Party has killed innocent people before," I said.

The crowd agreed and people cursed the government. One of them
said, "If only the Chinese people had weapons, we would fight our

way into Zhongnanhai and kill them all. But we don't have any weapons."

When we finished talking and I started to move off, a young man came up beside me, took hold of my elbow, and said in a low voice, "You ought to be careful now. They're already many plainclothes security police on the campus." I thanked him for his concern and we both said *baozhong*, "Be careful," as we parted.

Many new, large, black-lettered slogans were up now:

"Down with Li Peng. If Li doesn't fall, the workers won't stand for it."

"Wan Li: call an emergency session of the National People's Congress." Wan was a member of the Politburo, the chairman of the National People's Congress and widely regarded as a reformer.

"Long live democracy!"

"Use violence against a violent government."

"The democratic fighters are dead but not finished."

"Death to the Li-Yang Clique!"

Reports were coming over the loudspeakers. One eyewitness said, "Last night (Sunday night, June 4) tanks ran over thirteen students, killed about 30 workers and many other people including an old woman who was kneeling in front of them begging them to stop. Soon after that, some soldiers were grabbed and killed by people who had witnessed the shooting of the old woman. Another old woman was wounded in the leg while sleeping in her second-story apartment."

The student said he saw the wound—a big piece of her calf was blown away. It was the only story I heard involving tanks on the evening of June 4, and it's possible he got the date wrong. But it could have been part of the street fighting after the massacre.

Eleven injured Peking University students were in the nearby Xi Yuan Hospital of Chinese Medicine, the broadcaster said. He asked professors and fellow students to visit them.

After riding twenty minutes in the direction of the Summer Palace, I found the hospital. I realized I had been there with my students several times in 1986–87, but had not known the hospital's formal name. After inquiring in several offices, I found the ward where the students were supposed to be, but the hospital officials wouldn't let me in.

The nurses on duty were suspicious of a foreigner, even though I could prove I was from Peking University. An older woman who looked worn-out and despondent said there were no Beida students there: "We had some here yesterday, but they're all gone now." As I turned to leave, a younger nurse said in a deadpan voice, "If you want to see them, you'll have to come back during visiting hours after two o'clock."

At the Shaoyuan complex around 11 A.M., people were walking around anxiously in front of the main building and on the steps of Building Number Five. Everyone, students and scholars alike, were waiting for the army. We feared the worst would happen when they arrived. I was told the Japanese Embassy had already telephoned their students at Shaoyuan and advised them to stay inside. They thought troops were on their way to the university that day.

Most of the "foreign experts" at Shaoyuan couldn't speak Chinese and did not know what was going on. An American woman who had accompanied her lecturer husband was extremely distraught. They had recently arrived, and nobody on the Chinese side had even suggested it might be dangerous for them to come. She wanted badly to get out of there before the shooting started—nobody doubted there would be shooting—but their hosts assured them they would guarantee their safety.

It didn't appear that anything concerning the Chinese army could be guaranteed, especially not by university authorities. We were also told by another foreigner working with the Geography Department that the department chairman had told him the president of Peking University was negotiating with the army commanders for a peaceful takeover.

Shortly after lunch the French Embassy evacuated all French students from Shaoyuan in two minibuses. A member of the evacuation team told me the embassy determined that the universities weren't safe, and they were taking the students to the embassy compound. They could stay with staff workers for a few days until things settled down.

At that point I went up to my room and phoned an emergency number for the United States Embassy; the number had been mailed to registered American citizens, like myself, when martial law was declared. The man who answered my call said the embassy had no policy statement at this time except that I should stay in my "hotel" room. He said the embassy was very concerned and had made the security of American citizens its first priority. President Bush had even called the embassy that morning and a meeting was to begin soon to decide on an official policy. The official told me to call back at 2 P.M.

I phoned the Canadian Embassy, whose representative said they were going to evacuate their students from Beida that afternoon, and that they would have a minibus at the Friendship Hotel at 2:30 to pick up other Canadian nationals. I should bring only one small bag because the bus was small and they were taking us to stay temporarily at the residences of Canadian Embassy staff personnel.

Then I made a fatal mistake: I told them I was only a "landed immigrant"–what U.S. citizens would call a permanent resident–and not a Canadian citizen, but that my wife was a Canadian citizen. The voice at the other end grew cold, and the man said he was "very sorry, but you'll have to apply to the U.S. Embassy for assistance. If our bus is full, we cannot take you." So much for the "hands across border" tripe. When push comes to shove, it's every man for himself.

Foreign experts and students were gathering in front of the main building. The Peking University Office of Foreign Student Affairs was arranging for a university minibus to pick up American students who were attending the University of California's program at Beida. T. Y. Shen, their resident director and a professor at Berkeley, was trying to persuade the office to hire a full-size bus so other Americans could also leave. But the office said they couldn't find another bus driver willing to risk the drive across town to the hotel area, let alone one who would drive to the even more dangerous embassy district. For once I don't think they were lying.

Shen was also in contact with the American Embassy. They told him they'd call after 2:30, when their meeting ended and they had an official policy. They didn't. He managed to contact the embassy again after 3 P.M., and they said they'd send "a vehicle" to pick up American citizens about 4:30.

The temperature was about 90 degrees in the courtyard. A dozen of us dragged all of our bags out there and began the long wait for the promised transportation. We watched wistfully as the Beida minibus took the California students away. There was no extra room on their bus, not even for the American woman who was so anxious to leave.

Half an hour later, a small black car pulled up. An African student and a Chinese woman started to load his bags in the trunk. Several of us had the same thought: there was room for one more. There wasn't enough room for the American woman and her husband, so I flipped a coin with another American who wanted to leave then. Fate elected me to join the lucky pair in what I discovered was a Peking University car hired for this Guyanaian student by the Office of Foreign Student Affairs. I loaded on my two extremely heavy suitcases and hopped in the back. The young woman was a student from another university who had come to Beida for a graduate seminar a few days ago and got stuck there. She lived near the Lidu Hotel, the Beijing Holiday Inn, on Capital Airport Road, where the Guyanaian student's embassy had advised him to go.

As we drove slowly out of campus and made our way toward the Second Circle Road, the Guyanaian said his friends at the Beijing Language Institute had seen troops come onto campus Sunday. They ordered everyone to stay inside and not go outdoors. When several students, men and women, went out of their building to see what was happening, they were immediately gunned down. The Chinese woman had also heard of similar incidents at Beijing Medical College and People's University, but not from eyewitnesses. The more we talked the safer we felt, I suppose, so we kept up a constant chatter, until we came to the roadblock.

A major intersection was blocked off by two double-size city buses across each of the four roads. We edged together with a long line of delivery trucks, bicycles and other vehicles, and went through a car-size gap between two buses. We were in the center of the intersection, within the roadblock, and it reminded me of being in a circle of covered wagons in an old Western. Young people sat in all of the buses; it seemed to me they were waiting for the army to break through this main thoroughfare leading to the university district. Slogans painted on the buses read, "Hang the executioner Li Peng!" and "Repay a debt of blood with blood!"

We inched along, expecting to go through a similar gap on the other side. Then the trucks in front stopped and began turning around. There was no corresponding gap.

At that moment we heard the frightening noise of a military helicopter hovering overhead. This is it, I thought, we've had it. They're going to start shooting. We shouted at the driver to turn the hell around and get out of there. But as a model citizen of the socialist society, this middle-aged gentleman was in no hurry to risk denting the university's car. Who would pay the repair bill? I shouted that if he didn't turn faster, he'd better let me drive. Finally he came slowly around and started back the wrong way, on the left side of the road until we could find a break in the cement divider between the lanes.

We considered going north onto the Third Circle Road, but there seemed to be large crowds at every intersection. In the end we decided to return to Beida. It was far better to be stuck there than somewhere totally unprotected.

We got back to Shaoyuan at about 5 P.M. A bus from the Canadian Embassy had taken their students away less than five minutes earlier, and they had actually taken two non-Canadians – the American lecturer and his wife.

Still no sign of the promised American vehicle.

A caravan of eleven shiny black cars drove in, made a grand sweep in front of the steps, and parked across the lawn from the main building. They were from the West German Embassy and they were evacuating all their students from Peking University. We asked if they could take six or seven Americans with them, but they still had to visit three more campuses and pick up at least 25 more students. Obviously they wouldn't have room for us, but their presence gave the lie to the U.S. Embassy's claim that they couldn't pick us up because there weren't any vehicles. If the Germans have eleven black cars, we murmured resentfully, how many must the Americans have?

We waited for that "vehicle" until 7 P.M., when the embassy phoned one of us and said they weren't coming that day. We should phone Tuesday after ten o'clock. After ten? But the Chinese army seemed to prefer attacking unarmed civilians in the predawn hours!

By then several large tour buses from the Shangri-la Hotel had pulled up out front. The drivers said they were waiting for the Japanese students to finish packing. I decided to go back to my room.

I'd just finished hauling my 60-pound suitcases up the five flights to my room when one of the other fellowship-holders, let's call him Zhao, phoned and said I ought to leave campus that night. He was a Chinese-American who had been in Beijing for more than a year working on a research project.

"The Japanese are evacuating their people, and it has been my experience that the Japanese always do the right thing in such situations," he said. "They're very cautious and they're usually very well-informed. If they think the army's coming tonight, they may be right."

A Japanese friend was sure he could persuade the Japanese to take us along. "Besides, the Japanese love the Americans," he said.

I hesitated a moment, thinking about the weight of my baggage and how I hated to drag them up and down the stairs if I didn't have to. "Okay, let's go," I said.

The Japanese "loved" these two Americans better than the American Embassy did. With Zhao's help carrying one of my suitcases, we loaded ourselves into an air-conditioned bus chartered by the Japanese government, and made the ten-minute trip to the Shangri- la Hotel.

An American television cameraman and his young Chinese

assistant had been filming our exodus and other things around campus through the afternoon. Since their headquarters were in the Shangri-la they hitched a ride when the buses reached the South Gate. The Chinese newsman was an instant celebrity with several other Chinese at the Shangri-la.

And here's how legends are born. The assistant described how troops lined up in front of the students on the square and opened fire with their automatic weapons. So much was true. But he said that before they fired, the handsome young student leader Wuer Kaixi stepped out from the crowd to talk to them. Unable to persuade them to let the students go, Wuer Kaixi said, "If you want to shoot, then go on, shoot!" He stood with his arms outstretched, bearing his chest, and went down in a hail of gunfire.

"Are you sure Wuer Kaixi was killed?" I asked.

"Yes. He's dead. They've already had a memorial service for him at Beijing Normal."

Zhao and I checked into the Shangri-la, in a double room. Not until we turned on the television and watched the Cable News Network reports did I realize how bad things really were at Tiananmen and what danger we might be in. There were row after row of tanks on the Avenue of Eternal Peace, troops everywhere from Xidan to Jianguomenwai, and pictures of an enraged crowd setting fire to a row of army trucks. Add to that the news of demonstrations taking place all across China, rumors of fighting between troops of the 27th Army (branded as responsible for the massacre) and the local 38th Army, and the reports indicating a real possibility of civil war. If civil war broke out, or even if two armies battled in Beijing, the airport would be closed and we'd be trapped for the duration.

Since both of us had participated in illegal demonstrations after the declaration of martial law, we figured we'd better leave the country the next day. After a late dinner, we arranged for a taxi to take us to the airport at 9 A.M. Tuesday.

Several young Chinese were seated on sofa chairs in the hallway, talking quietly. They lived nearby and had come over to watch the American television news in the room of a Chinese-American businessman. As I walked closer, I noticed one of them was handing out what looked like photocopied photographs. People would look at them hastily, and put them in their pockets, so I didn't get a good look. When I spoke to them in Chinese, however, the owner of the originals let me see them: three or four pictures of students' mutilated bodies. They had been shot down in the streets the day before.

I told them the foreign news broadcasts reported that the 27th Army was regrouping in a defensive formation in anticipation of a possible attack by the 38th Army. The person who took the pictures then said with a mixture of sadness and fury, "They deserve to be killed. They killed too many people, killed too many people."

Back in our room, Zhao phoned friends in Hong Kong to let them know he was safe, and to see if they could buy him a plane ticket out of Beijing. I already had a JAL ticket, which I could exchange at the airport.

I tried to phone my wife in Vancouver, but all the overseas lines to North America were tied up. Then I had a brainstorm: from the Shangri-la it was possible to dial directly to Taiwan. I called my sister-in-law in Taipei, got through right away, and asked her to call Vancouver and give my wife my number. When Josephine called, I told her we were going to the airport the following morning. She said the Canadian Broadcasting Corporation's "Early Edition" wanted to call me around midnight Beijing time for a radio interview.

Zhao and I were dead tired, but we were also nervous wondering about our chances of making it to the airport. We didn't get much sleep that night either. "Early Edition" called and I said we'd left Peking University because everyone thought it was unsafe there. I also said I thought there would be a civil war in China. (It turned out that the reports about civil war being imminent were exaggerated. But I have heard eyewitnesses talk of fighting between military units immediately after the massacre.)

I also passed along the story that Wuer Kaixi had been killed. This also was untrue, I learned later.

"Professor Duke, how do you feel being there now? How do you feel about what has happened since the last couple of days?" the interviewer asked.

It was like asking me how I felt about a death in the family. I nearly broke down. "I feel sick. I've seen the youth of China die and I just feel terrible. I mean, what else can I feel? It's very sad."

I criticized President Bush's first statements as being insufficiently forceful, and said there should be "some kind of punitive action" by the western democracies.

The interview was picked up by several other Canadian news services; they kept calling me all night. The last call came about 4 A.M.

Tuesday morning we checked out of the hotel and waited for our taxi to show up. By then I had consolidated all of my necessary material into one suitcase and one plastic bag from the hotel. I had thrown away two-thirds of my clothes, some books, and my tape recorder. I deliberately abandoned the seventeen cassette tapes I had made of speeches from the Beida Student Broadcast Station, information on big-character posters, demonstration sounds and conversations. I had not recorded names, so they couldn't get anyone in trouble. Zhao and I had torn up all our propaganda leaflets and flushed them down the toilet the night before.

We left for the airport at 9 A.M., after agreeing to pay the driver $150 Chinese in foreign exchange certificates, which was $40 U.S. at the official rate or about $69 U.S. on the black market. He assured us the road was clear; he had already been there once this morning. We would take the same Second Circle Road that was blockaded on Monday.

The roadblock was gone. The city looked just like a war zone, worse than Watts but not as bad as Beirut. Abandoned or burned out buses and trucks littered the roadside, but the road itself was free of obstructions.

Somewhere east of the Lama Temple, we were stopped at a military roadblock manned by a platoon of armed soldiers. A young officer looked us over and asked the driver where we were going. He replied he was taking these foreigners to the airport and we held up our American passports. The officer ignored us and ordered the driver to turn around and go back.

So they're not letting people go to the airport, we thought. It would be safer to wait at the Shangri-la. We had several hundred dollars in cash and travelers checks, as well as my American Express card and two Visa cards. We could have stayed for a month, but we were uneasy about getting caught in the middle of a Chinese civil war. Or, which was more likely, a nasty situation where the unpredictable government or army decides to make an example of some foreigners, say American citizens who had joined in illegal demonstrations. We remembered a number of Americans who spent years in Chinese jails for similar reasons.

Cable News and other programs that day didn't make us feel any safer. A military expert from a Washington think tank interviewed on "Good Morning America" said the Chinese army's chain of command had broken down and anything could happen. Network programs showed the 27th Army in its defensive formation, as if it expected an attack by other army units, not by civilians. Traffic was paralyzed in Shanghai, and both that city and Nanjing were reported surrounded by army units awaiting orders to enter. The Beijing airport was a scene of panic, and Dan Rather was making histrionic comments about catching "the last plane from Beijing."

We grew up watching Americans escape from Saigon or get trapped in Teheran, but now we were in the evening news ourselves, not sitting home watching it during dinner.

I called Josephine and told her we couldn't get out but would keep trying. Meanwhile, she had been phoning officials of the United States and Canada, trying to find out if they planned to help Americans leave China. They didn't.

Later in the afternoon, I finally got through to the American Embassy. It's hard to believe there was only one number for all their extensions. The man at the other end said they still had no plans to evacuate U.S. nationals, but personally, if he had a choice, he'd leave if at all possible. He promised to pass along our names and room number to the American Citizens' Service Committee. If the policy changed the embassy would contact us. They never did.

After dinner, I ran into a group of American tourists who had just arrived two days before without any warning about what was going on. They had been abandoned by their guide, who was living in a hotel downtown. Monday afternoon they had taken a minibus to the CAAC ticket counter at Shatan, about a mile and a half from Tiananmen Square, to buy tickets for Guangzhou.

They said the CAAC computers were down and they couldn't buy the tickets, but they planned to go the next day and try again. I couldn't believe it. "Don't you know what's going on down there?" I asked. "It's a war zone. Turn on your TV and take a look!"

They said their tour guide had instructed them to proceed to Guangzhou. From there they could take a train to Hong Kong.

This is the cheapest way to leave China in normal times, and the tour guide seemed to be trying to save her company some money. But I told them they'd be crazy to go to the ticket counter downtown or fly to Guangzhou. "It's still in China, you know," I said.

Later I tried to call several friends to say good-bye. I had a long conversation with the wife of a journalist friend, who was a reporter herself. She said troops were marching at all hours of the day and night since June 4. On Monday they had deliberately fired into their building, the Jianguomenwai foreign residents compound.

I couldn't reach all my friends at Peking University, but I managed to contact one of them. We both choked up when I told him to take care of himself, and he actually said, "We have treated you badly."

"No, no, no, you just take care."

"We'll certainly meet again," he said.

"Yes, I believe we will."

Zhao and I spent another restless night in the hotel room. His friends in Hong Kong had heard reports that Chinese from Hong Kong were being stopped at the Beijing airport and refused permission to leave, and were taken away by security police. Several of his friends called him throughout the night to make sure he was safe and see if he had any more information. He assured them he wasn't among those stopped, and besides he was an American citizen. Nothing could happen to him—or could it? After all, he had marched in demonstrations and been to Tiananmen often. By then he was pretty scared too.

I had fallen into a troubled and sweaty sleep when Josephine called me at 4:30 A.M. Wednesday, and urged me to get started for the airport. In her anxiety, she had misjudged the time difference.

Since I was up, I called the U.S. Embassy's 24-hour hotline. A woman answered this time, a volunteer, and said the American government was evacuating embassy dependents and advising all American nationals to leave the country immediately. But they still had no plans to get us to the airport. She told of many ingenious ways to make it to the airport, such as a four-hour trek in a pedicab. Her husband took someone to the airport the day before in a car and it took only the usual 30 to 40 minutes. He had no trouble at all. He had gone down the same road where we were stopped by the army roadblock.

I told her about the American tourists who planned to go to the CAAC office, and she agreed it would be a foolhardy move. She said I'd "be doing them a great service" if I would persuade them to go directly to the airport and fly out of China. Also, the more of us there were in a group the better our chances of getting to the airport.

The information desk gave me the names and room numbers of this last American tour group; we met at 8 A.M., after breakfast. Most of them were ready to take my advice, but two were holding out. They finally decided to go with us after Josephine called again from Vancouver and said she had been told all local flights in China were now canceled. This proved to be incorrect, but it did the trick.

Well before 9 A.M., we left for the airport in a taxi and a minibus. The minibus I was in was driven by an enterprising fellow who charged us $150 U.S. (ten times the usual rate), payable only if he actually got us there. This time we made it with no trouble. We passed the same burned-out vehicles and saw a large number of troops bivouacked just east of the Airport Road, but there were no frightening incidents.

There was really no panic at the airport. Beijing Capital Airport is badly run in the best of times, so it was a total mess now, with thousands of people trying to leave at the same time. Zhao and I signed up on a waiting list for two extra United Airlines flights put on the day before, but we were numbers 147 and 148. We had no chance of getting on today's flight. The next flight was scheduled for Friday and we didn't relish the idea of staying overnight in the airport.

Our best bet was to buy a ticket to Hong Kong from good old CAAC. There was a long Chinese-style line-up in front of the government airline's ticket counter. That is, it was three to five people across and ten yards long, continually increasing at the front, rather than the back. But we got lucky.

Another Japanese friend of Zhao's who had lived in China for several years told us we'd never make it waiting in line that way. So a group of six of us from Peking University filled out our ticket applications, gave them to him along with our passports and money, and he simply strong-armed his way to the front like any self-respecting PRC citizen and bought our tickets for us. The ticket-sellers couldn't care less how their customers appeared at the front. It took him only an hour, and we all had tickets on an Air China flight scheduled to leave for Hong Kong at 1:30.

After a horrendous baggage foul-up, standard operating procedure for China, we made it through customs to the boarding area. Zhao and I were particularly worried about going through the passport check, imagining the security police with photos or videos of all foreigners who spent time on Tiananmen Square or walked in illegal demonstrations.

I had shaved my full beard down to a goatee, and discarded the red-and-white baseball cap I wore all the time in the Beijing sun. Now I pretended I didn't understand Chinese.

We got to the boarding gate without a hitch, but Zhao insisted there were bound to be plainclothes security police there. He became agitated when I watched a television in the waiting room. It was a press conference by Yuan Mu, an official spokesman, lately known as China's Geobbels. Yuan was ranting about how the "counter-revolutionary hooligans" and "dregs of society" had destroyed hundreds of trucks and buses. He never mentioned the tanks and APCs.

"Do you know how much of the people's money a bus or a truck costs?" he said, and went on to quote the figures. I grew angry listening to him and started to say something about him to Zhao, but he stopped me with a worried look. He whispered that I should not let on that I understood Chinese. He was apprehensive that as an ethnic Chinese he might be prevented from boarding the plane. I didn't feel very safe either, so I held my tongue.

After another seemingly endless wait, we boarded the plane about 3:30. Then we had to sit there for an hour without air conditioning. After half an hour the chief steward announced in Chinese and English that they were waiting for six passengers who arrived late and had not yet made it through customs. We didn't believe him at first, but then several more people did come aboard.

A few minutes later the steward said in Mandarin only that one passenger had failed to get on, and that a small black bag had been left on board. He requested that everybody check their carry-on baggage to see if there was an extra unidentified bag among them. Bomb scare, we thought, as we quickly checked the overhead compartment. We noticed we were the only ones checking.

The crew didn't seem to be checking for anything. Then we began to think out loud. How could there be a black bag inside the plane if the missing passenger hadn't even boarded? Why were they delaying the flight? Was the airport going to be closed now that we had finally made it onto a plane? Were Chinese planes going to be refused permission to leave? If they really thought there was a bomb on the plane, they would have to check the luggage compartment, which was right under our seats. That could take hours.

They didn't search it. They didn't do anything, in fact. A few minutes later, after we had been on the plane about an hour, we began to taxi to our takeoff runway. Nothing more was said about the missing passenger or the black bag.

I had visions of the plane exploding somewhere on the way to Hong Kong after the jet reached the altitude needed to activate some sort of detonator. And we were right on top of the baggage compartment. At least it would be over quickly. I fingered the silver cross my wife always gives me to carry when I fly, and prayed it would not happen. If it did, I prayed I would fare as well as the heroes in Salman Rushdie's *Satanic Verses*.

The flight was uneventful and at about seven o'clock local time we landed in Hong Kong, still part of the free world for another seven years. After booking a seat on Cathay Pacific's 10 A.M. daily flight direct to Vancouver the next day, I went to the Hotel Fortuna where I knew they'd have CNN news. I called Josephine and said I'd be home at 7 A.M. on June 8.

Among the calls I made in Hong Kong was one to Mr. and Mrs.

Lam Shan-muk of the paper *Xin bao.* Like others, they had called Vancouver several times asking about my safety. I told them the rumor that Wuer Kaixi had been killed on Tiananmen Square and a memorial service had been held at Beijing Normal University. Lam asked me to write something for *Xin bao* and I promised to do my best.

On June 8, I flew on Cathay Pacific Flight 800 direct from Kai Tak Airport in Hong Kong to Vancouver. We took off at 10:15 A.M. and arrived at 7 A.M. the same morning, Vancouver time.

I learned that the day after we managed to leave Beijing, Perry Link, the director of the Committee for Scholarly Communication, had gone to the Shangri-la Hotel in a CSC car to take us to the airport. I also heard that Wuer Kaixi was not shot in Tiananmen Square after all. He later described the way he collapsed and was taken away in an ambulance early on June 4. It's not surprising that rumors of his death would circulate and be passed along by everyone, myself included.

A platoon of TV and radio reporters were at the airport. I was asked if I thought I'd return to China.

"Not until the present government falls from power," I said. "I would like to think that I will not return to China until a monument is erected in Tiananmen Square to the students and workers who were killed there."

CHAPTER 11

THE PURGE

FTER THE TIANANMEN MASSACRE, THE PURGE spread. All indications are that the disaster is just beginning. The massacre was the first step in a campaign to systematically eliminate all the gains made by Chinese society in the past ten years.

There have been mass arrests. Many of China's most talented artists, writers and professionals have fled into foreign exile. Thousands of students who were overseas during the crackdown are afraid to go home. Others are in hiding.

On July 20 a group of exiles in Paris—including the student leader Wuer Kaixi, Yan Jiaqi, Stone Computer director Wan Runnan, political theorist Su Shaozhi, and Liu Bin yan—released a statement on the purge. According to information given to them by "a Beijing official sympathetic to the Democracy Movement" and based on internal documents the official had obtained, more than 120,000 democracy supporters had been arrested throughout China. In Beijing alone more than 10,000 had been arrested and 20,000 called in for questioning.

This source also said more than 100 secret executions had taken place. There were 27 publicly announced executions, all of them workers, during the first weeks of the purge.

Arrests, tortures and secret executions seem to be continuing. In the first week in September, Amnesty International sent a telex to Premier Li Peng urging an end of secret executions. Based on past experience, this human rights group believes the Chinese government will continue to summarily execute many persons charged with what it regards as "most serious crimes," while periodically announcing only as many executions as it believes necessary to terrorize the public.

In what the Beijing people call the "black terror," the Public Security Bureau police arrive in the middle of the night, surround a neighborhood compound or an apartment building, and warn the public not to come outside or try to see what is happening. This is none of your business, they say. Then they knock on doors and ask for particular suspects, or just barge in. When they find somebody they want they simply grab him and take him away.

In early September they were picking up people at random in areas where ordinary citizens had stopped the army. Some of the victims weren't actually involved in that.

When they take someone to the police station they beat, torture and humiliate him. They make him lie face down on the floor as if to do push-ups and beat him on the buttocks with their nightsticks. The victim is not supposed to cry out, or he will be beaten all the more severely. So he must cover his mouth to keep from screaming.

Of course, all this is in addition to the terrible bloodshed during the crackdown. And just how bloody it was, nobody can say with certainty.

Undoubtedly we can discount the official sources. In a June 6 press conference, government spokesman Yuan Mu said only 23 students and approximately 300 soldiers, rioters and bystanders were killed. More than 5,000 officers and soldiers were injured, he said.

In an American television interview ten days later, he claimed there were no casualties at Tiananmen and nobody was killed. On another occasion he claimed army vehicles didn't run over one single person.

A more reliable estimate comes from an army medic who was on the square that night. He told a relative, a student at the University of Law and Government, that at least 1,600 student corpses could be counted on the square that morning, not counting those whose bodies were so horribly crushed that it was impossible to tell how many there were. The account was passed along to the *Wenhuibao* of Hong Kong, which printed it.

As early as 2 A.M. on June 4, while the massacre was continuing, the Chinese Red Cross announced that more than 2,000 students and townspeople had been killed. The organization was later forced to recant.

Contention, a Hong Kong magazine reputed to have extremely good connections with the Chinese Communist Party hierarchy, claimed that reliable sources put the total at 10,440 civilians killed and 28,790 wounded from June 3 through June 9. The toll in soldiers was placed at 17 dead and 2,043 wounded. There is no way to confirm the accuracy of these numbers. They seem rather high, but nevertheless more likely than the government's figures.

I think it is reasonable to believe that at least 2,000 people were killed on the Avenue of Eternal Peace and in Tiananmen Square.

I often think of the beautiful, dirty *waidi* kids – the outside-Beijing students – who occupied the square. News accounts say most of those slaughtered were *waidi*. In late May, the demonstrations were starting to peter out and many of the local students were going back to class. But the *waidi* voted to stay in Tiananmen. They had just arrived. They'd never seen the city sights before and they might not make it back again. So in the last week before the massacre, most of the people in the square were students from outside Beijing, plus a large contingent of militant young workers from the Independent Workers' Union.

Most heartbreaking was the report that many of the *waidi* ran into the underground street crossings when the army moved in. They thought the APCs couldn't reached them, but there they were the easiest possible targets. Jammed together in the tunnels, they were cut down by waves of machine-gun bullets.

An indication that the killing was widespread is that the government paid hefty and unprecedented compensation for people "killed accidentally."

Nobody could have been killed accidentally on the street if the government's version of what happened were true. The martial law command had given orders for everyone to remain indoors or suffer the consequences. If you were out on the street and killed by soldiers in the line of duty, while they were putting down a counter-revolution, then it was your fault.

A knowledgeable Chinese friend suggested that these dead were plainclothes police. They were out spying on the students, got caught in the chaos of the army's killing spree, and were gunned down. Their families threatened to make a stink about it unless the government compensated them handsomely, my friend suspects.

Can we believe the government's claim that 300 soldiers were killed putting down this "rebellion"? I think not. CCTV propaganda continually showed the same burned and mangled bodies of a dozen soldiers killed by the angry crowds. If hundreds were killed, more would have been shown.

A friend of mine who was in Beijing from May to October both witnessed the massacre and watched the government's doctored videotapes. He told me the government simply reversed the events of June 3 and 4. They showed people burning vehicles and attacking the APCs on the fourth while a voice-over said it was the third. Then they showed the troops, their "patience" exhausted, peacefully dispersing the crowd.

An estimated 150,000 to 200,000 troops from all across China were called up to surround the capital. Not all of them participated in the massacre. Although the 27th Army is believed to have done most of the killing, many different groups may have been involved. According to some reports, one unit was chosen to participate from each of the many armies—perhaps a regiment here and a company there. That way, the responsibility was spread throughout the military system.

A young man recently out of the army said he met an army friend of his in Beijing several days after the massacre. In surprise he asked, "What are you doing here, did you . . . ?"

Before he could finish the question, his friend interjected, "No, no, I wasn't in on it. Some troops from our army went to Tiananmen, but my unit wasn't sent in." In other words, he was saying, "I did not kill anyone."

Given the hatred the people of Beijing now have for anyone in uniform, it is not surprising this young man would immediately disclaim any personal responsibility for the massacre. But a Chinese friend of mine from Beijing believes there is another even more important reason for such a young soldier to be afraid. Given the ruthless nature of the regime and its desperate desire to hide the truth of the massacre *from the rest of the armed forces*, he said, the troops who did the actual killing are now in grave danger of being done away with by the leadership.

It would be quite easy for the authorities to divide these soldiers into small units and eliminate them in a number of different ways. They could kill them in practice maneuvers, stage some kind of an accident, send them across the Vietnam border on a suicidal mission, or transfer them to far-flung border areas and never let them come back. This seems inconceivable to us, but few Chinese I know would doubt the present regime's ability to do such things if they thought it necessary to maintain their power.

In the spring of 1987, after the previous democracy demonstrations were shut down as part of the anti-bourgeois liberalization campaign, hard-liners prepared a hit list. At that time, they merely wrote down names. Now they are methodically going after the people they despise most, the finest minds in China.

The hit list was a rumor when I was in Beijing, but the children of a famous scholar told me in a telephone conversation in July that their parents' names were definitely on such a list.

Many famous writers, scholars and economic experts have been arrested.

Virtually the entire media leadership was purged when Tianjin's Mayor Li Ruihuan took charge of propaganda in July. The editorial departments of *People's Daily*, *Guangming Daily*, *China's Legal System* and *Technology Daily* have been decimated, as have those of television and radio stations. Top editors and managers have been fired or transferred and their reporting staffs have been forced to undergo severe questioning, with armed soldiers present, about their actions.

Liang Xiang, Provincial Governor of Hainan Island, whom the students said was disassociating himself from the government, was removed from office sometime before the middle of September. He was charged with corruption but the real reason for his dismissal seems to be that he ordered the Hainan party members to practice restraint in dealing with the demonstrators.

After the massacre, the government claimed that the dissident Fang Lizhi was a prime instigator of the student movement. That simply is not true. The prime motivation for the movement came from the students' own experiences of life in China.

It may be true, however, as several intellectuals told me later, that some student leaders went to visit Fang's wife, Li Shuxian, to ask for her advice after the demonstrations began. That was perfectly normal because she was the elected political representative from the Haidian district which includes Peking University.

Fang and Li Shuxian, surely among the regime's version of the "Ten Most Wanted," sought refuge in the American Embassy in Beijing. They are still there, as of this writing.

Of the 33 prominent intellectual figures who had signed an open letter supporting Fang Lizhi's letter of January 16, many are now under arrest, being criticized by name as supporters of the "counter-revolution" or have fled the country after warrants were issued for their arrest.

Among the 42 scientists and intellectuals who signed an open letter to Zhao Ziyang and others on Feb. 26, the whereabouts of some like Bao Zunxin have been unknown since June 4, while others such as Zhang Xianyang are being criticized by name at the time of this writing—meaning they are in desperate trouble.

On March 14, another letter supporting Fang's position was signed by 43 writers. Addressing the National People's Congress, they also called for amnesty for all political prisoners. This letter was organized by Dai Qing, the reporter for the *Guangming Daily* who later tried to negotiate to get the students out of Tiananmen.

After the crackdown, Dai publicly renounced her membership in the Chinese Communist Party, and she was arrested in mid-July. She was charged with aiding the "rebellion" through her journalism in support of the Democracy Movement, and was being held for several months in the infamous Qin Cheng Prison outside Beijing. A close friend of hers, now in exile, told me she would not be executed, but despite her many connections she would suffer all of the indignities and humiliations of prison life. She was released from prison briefly early in November, but was soon returned to prison, where she now remains.

Another of the letter's signers, Yan Jiaqi, is now in Paris after narrowly escaping arrest as a principal architect of the "rebellion." In September he was elected chairman of the Federation of Democracy in China.

Liu Xiaopo, an intellectual who was famous for his spirited attacks on the flaws in Chinese culture, is in custody and has been badly beaten. A Lanzhou University student named Xin Ku, who is now studying at Yale, managed to escape after the crackdown. In Toronto he said that Liu had been beaten so severely he could not straighten his back. Liu was sent to the hospital to recover, because the regime hopes to force him to make false statements.

After the massacre, high-ranking managerial types such as Yan Zhun, general manager of Deng Pufang's Kanghua-Longsheng Corporation, chose to leave China. In Europe this September, he told reporters he would rather be "a wandering exile with no nationality. Personally," he went on, "I have nothing to worry about. The Communist Party has treated me well." Nevertheless, he gave up his "special political privileges, high cadre emoluments, and comfortable life and work" because "inscribed on my banner are the words humanity and conscience."

During the marathon get-together of the intellectuals who always supported each other during times of crisis, these old friends predicted disaster for Zhao's reform group. They were right.

Many of Zhao's followers in all departments have been purged. In September, Chen Yizi, a close advisor to Zhao who is now in France, told reporters in Paris that at least fourteen members of Zhao's Commission on Restructuring the Economic System have been arrested, while others would be sent to border provinces for "labor reform."

Later reports said the commission was disbanded and most of its 100 member were sent off to remote parts of China.

Some well-known economic reformers either fled the country or disappeared after warrants were issued for their arrests. Two executives of the highly-successful Stone Computer Corporation are a good example: Wan Runnan is in exile in Paris, while Cao Siyuan has been arrested. A famous young intellectual, Su Xiaokang, escaped to Paris after 100 days in hiding.

On July 2, the Chinese Academy of Social Sciences—the group with which I marched in a protest demonstration—came out in favor of everything the government had done. But this kind of coerced support is meaningless.

That same month, Beijing Mayor Chen Xitong released a long report blaming the movement for "bourgeois liberalization" on Zhao and his followers. At the same time, another spokesman attacked Hu Jiwei, the 72-year-old former editor of People's Daily, for heading a petition drive to call an extraordinary session of the National People's Congress, in which it would impeach Premier Li Peng. The People's Congress has the constitutional authority to do this, but has never made such a move.

Hu continued to maintain that his actions were completely in accord with the Chinese Constitution. He refused to make a self-criticism or acknowledge any wrongdoing.

The overseas Chinese press reported during the first week of September that Culture Minister Wang Meng was formally removed from office. He was said to be the only official of ministerial rank who did not make a public visit to "console and congratulate" the martial law troops.

What happened to the people I knew or saw?

One of the two low-spirited professors who came to my room in late May had invited me to his house "after things settle down a bit." He never did and I never saw either of them again.

In the days before the massacre, a great deal of media propaganda was made out of the ink-throwing incident I witnessed, in which Mao's giant portrait was defaced.

Afterwards, according to Asiaweek, a 25-year-old primary school teacher from Hunan Province, Yu Zhijian, was sentenced to life imprisonment for splashing the picture with ink. Yu Dongyue, 22, a newspaper art editor, and Lu Decheng, 26, a transportation worker, were sentenced to twenty and sixteen years respectively.

I wonder if that wry student, who had kidded that they were off to "protect Zhongnanhai," is even still alive. His famous writer friend was arrested in late June or early July. As of this writing, he's still in prison.

During one march, I arranged to meet later for a longer talk with the leader of one of the departmental delegations to the demonstration. He was a famous scholar I'd wanted to meet for a long time. We were going to get together in late June. It never happened.

I worried about him for a long time after the massacre, especially because he was mentioned by name in Beijing Mayor Chen Xitong's "Report" on the incidents. No arrest warrant was issued, but this man had to be high on the hard-liners' list of intellectuals to be purged if they gained the upper hand. Later I learned that he managed to escape to Paris, along with many other intellectual exiles. He is now living in the United States.

And what of Xiao Luo, the peasant and small-time entrepreneur from whom I brought watermelons and oranges and with whom I traded foreign exchange certificates? I'm sure he's fine. His kind always survive. I feel confident he'll still be there in the Regional Agricultural Products Trade Center when this government falls and Josephine and I return to Beida.

§§§

After the bloodbath, the main concern of Peking University's administrators was the safety of their students, some of whom were planning to resist the takeover. Administrators and faculty were doubtless trying to buy time so they could discourage them from fighting and dying in hopeless battles.

Within a few days the university carried out its cleanup of campus, closing down the Student Broadcast Station, pulling down big-character posters, washing off slogans. No uniformed troops actually came onto the campus, but in the weeks that followed officers did come there several times in the early hours of the morning to search for and arrest students accused of "counter-revolution."

New enrollment in universities has been cut by 30,000, and Peking University was singled out for a 60 percent reduction, to just 800 entering freshmen. One witness told the foreign press that 40 Beida professors were seen cutting the grass on campus as part of the "thought reform" program.

Graduating seniors are being punished by arbitrary reassignment to unpopular jobs in the countryside.

In September, He Dongchang, the second Vice Minister of Education, announced a new policy to limit the number of graduate students studying in the United States and other western countries. It is necessary to place a "screen" over China's windows to the outside world, he said, to keep out the "flies and worms" that recently infested the country.

College students are now forced to take courses in Marxist theory. The 1989 entering freshman class is now spending a year in military training and indoctrination before they can start their university career.

According to an inner party report, called "Document Number Five," plans have been drawn up to send all young college graduates working in party or government organizations out into the countryside. News reporters and editors who graduated since 1985 are to spend one or two years in the rural life to strengthen their "party spirit." This would be a Cultural Revolution-type punishment.

If such a program is carried out—and there is still tremendous opposition to it in the party and the society—it would be the country's worst setback since the "up to the mountains, down to the countryside" movement of the 1960s and 1970s. Not content with killing off thousands of future intellectuals, the hard-liners are planning to sacrifice another generation of experts, the only people who are capable of creating a prosperous and livable modern society in China.

Under a new campaign that the people call "leniency on the outside and harshness on the inside," the government is doing everything possible to win back foreign investors and tourists—while enforcing a policy of testing and punishing the urban population. Under "Document Number Four," the population is divided into nineteen categories according to the seriousness of their crimes during the Democracy Movement. The first ten categories are to be "attacked" and punished as instigators— planners, top leaders, those who led the masses into blocking troops, people who attacked the soldiers or protected "counter-revolutionary elements" after the massacre, took weapons, etc. The next nine categories are to be "cleaned up" and rehabilitated. They are anyone who supported the movement, joined illegal organizations, spread rumors, and so on. Everyone must explain his activities to his work unit and give the correct answers to 24 questions about what he did during "the disturbance" in order to keep his job.

The party has repeatedly announced that China would continue its reforms, but obviously it is doing all it can to close the doors again after ten years of unprecedented openness.

The purge has not been carried out without resistance from the population. In Beijing the most obvious opposition has been the repeated armed attacks on Martial Law troops. Sporadic nighttime sniper attacks have continued ever since the massacre. More than 170 such attacks have been reported and some 212 soldiers have been assassinated, most of them while on night patrol duty. One officer was even grabbed, killed, and hidden in a deserted food warehouse in a suburban township of Beijing.

Another salient measure of resistance is the fact that of the seven intellectuals and 21 students for whom arrest warrants were issued in June only about half of them have definitely been arrested. Some of them have escaped with the aid of an "underground railroad" said to include Communist Party and Public Security Bureau officers. Others are still believed to be in hiding. Many other prominent purge targets have also escaped after as long as three months in hiding. This is truly unprecedented in the history of Communist Party government of China.

Many other forms of passive resistance have been reported. Most common is the usual form of simulating compliance by parroting the current line whenever required at study sessions or on university examinations. Despite police hotlines and pressure to turn in your friends and relatives, very few people are actively cooperating in the government's purge of their neighbors and fellow workers. This is especially true among intellectuals and professionals. In carrying out its purge of genuine intellectuals the ruling group will try to find some "cheap and shameless intellectuals" to speak on its behalf, but that is becoming increasingly difficult. Politburo member Song Ping complained in early September that many party units were not carrying out their assigned duties to punish supporters of the Democracy Movement. On October 18, 50 students and faculty members at Peking University stood up and walked out of a required political study class together in protest.

Workers are also reported to be practicing various forms of slowdown. Such slowdowns cannot always be distinguished from the increasingly frequent shutdown of state-run factories due to shortages of materials or electricity. Much of this passive resistance has the tacit approval of leadership units. This is especially true in the seacoast provinces. Officials in Guangdong Province regularly disregard in practice many orders issued from Beijing in spite of lip service compliance.

The workers are always the Chinese Communist Party's greatest fear. If they gain any autonomy from the party's control over their lives, then the system really might be finished.

Several weeks after the massacre, an official document came down for all work units to study. From then on, all the workers were supposed to "unify their thoughts" by studying and reciting the important speeches of Deng Xiaoping.

Under a massive campaign of thought control and ideological rectification, all the urban work units—in factories, businesses and schools—are required to participate in these political study sessions. Cultural Revolution rhetoric like "class struggle" and "red and expert" are back in vogue.

In the middle of August, the deputy director of the Beijing Workers' Autonomous Union, Yue Wu, surfaced in Paris after a warrant was issued for his arrest.

Yue has a long history of dealing with repression. During the Cultural Revolution he was imprisoned for five years for the crime of supporting the then-disgraced Deng Xiaoping. During that period his son died of measles because a hospital refused to treat the offspring of a "counter-revolutionary," and his wife went insane as a result.

As he began his exile, he told a reporter in Paris that, "The Chinese Communists are always afraid the workers will rise up in opposition. They could tolerate the student demonstrations for an entire month, but they would not allow the workers to demonstrate for one day. The workers always suffer most under a corrupt system, and thus," he concluded, "when the worker's opposition breaks out it will be tremendously powerful."

CHAPTER 12

REBUILDING THE IRON HOUSE

THE ULTIMATE HISTORICAL SIGNIFICANCE OF THE 1989 Democracy Movement will be determined by the influence it has on the future of China, by the role the movement plays in bringing about political democracy in China. However long that takes, the events of the spring of 1989 represent a turning point in the Chinese people's struggle for freedom and democracy.

For many reasons the 1989 Democracy Movement may be of greater historical significance than the May Fourth Movement of 1919, the April Fifth Movement of 1976, and the Democracy Wall or Peking Spring Movement of 1979.

It united the largest number of the most representative elements of Chinese urban society ever assembled in a completely spontaneous protest against dictatorship and for freedom, democracy, the rule of law, and human rights. It spread the most important theoretical ideas underlying the practice of democracy farther than ever before among the general population. They have learned lessons this spring that they will not easily forget.

The lines have now been drawn with utter clarity in full view of the global village, between, on the one hand, a ruthless party-state dictatorship concerned only with the preservation of its own power at any cost and a peaceful, nonviolent popular movement seeking to reform Chinese society.

It has brought about a further defection of those remaining intellectuals who put their faith in the Deng Xiaoping faction of the Communist Party. It has produced widespread alienation among urban workers, shopkeepers, teachers, middle-level functionaries, and ordinary people of all walks of life. It has increased the already great mistrust of the peasantry for the government. Many peasants did not immediately know what happened in Beijing, but millions of them will eventually learn the truth as a result of word-of-mouth information spread by those among them who regularly travel to the big cities.

It has brought about a political unity among the overseas Chinese community that has not been seen since the founding of the People's Republic and the Nationalist retreat to Taiwan. All over the world groups of overseas Chinese who have never before cooperated in any endeavor are beginning to abandon their petty rivalries in order to struggle for a common goal: freedom and democracy in China.

It has won the sympathy of millions of ordinary citizen-voters of the world's developed countries as well as the community of China scholars. This has put the political and business leaders of the western democracies in a position where they can no longer maintain the double standard of condemning every violation of human rights in the Soviet bloc while turning a blind eye to even greater violations that have taken place repeatedly in China over the past ten years. As the Soviet bloc continues to liberalize its societies, China's position will become even more untenable.

The Chinese Democracy Movement can now take its place as part of the mainstream of post-Communist dissident movements. Its leaders will now receive aid and publicity for their cause from the many elements of the democratic world which genuinely support the expansion of democratic political values and systems throughout the world.

The Beijing students' and workers' independent organizations were nominated for the Nobel Peace Prize. They did not receive it, but the Dalai Lama did—an obvious expression of condemnation for Chinese government repression. At the same time organizations like Asia Watch and Amnesty International have stepped up their efforts to inform the English-speaking world about human rights violations in China.

We should not underestimate the extremely important symbolic value of the Tiananmen Massacre itself. The slaughter of unarmed workers and students in the ceremonial heart of the nation, on the square where the nation's most important political symbolism unfolds, is an extremely powerful political symbol. This is well-known and greatly feared by the regime. It is another reason for the immediate invention of the Big Lie that there was no bloodbath on Tiananmen Square, that no one was killed on the square itself, especially not directly under the Monument to the Martyrs of the Revolution. This is why the regime hurriedly invited the hated foreign journalists to a photo-op session under the monument.

The Tiananmen Massacre, like the Gdansk shipyard strike or uprising in the township of Soweto, is now a symbol. And it will remain the most powerful symbol of the Chinese Democracy Movement from now on. The Chinese people, especially the people of Beijing, will never forget what the regime did there. The world will long remember the remarkable image of Wang Weilin standing alone and fearless in front of a column of tanks on the Avenue of Eternal Peace directly opposite Tiananmen.

The leaders of the current regime will always feel uneasy about what they ordered done there. Not because they feel repentant, but because on every national symbolic occasion in Tiananmen Square they can never be absolutely certain that some courageous Chinese citizen will not suddenly burst out of the crowd with a banner proclaiming "REMEMBER THE TIANANMEN MASSACRE!"

Each of these accomplishments represents significant progress for the 1989 Democracy Movement, progress that would not have been possible without the ultimate sacrifice of the people who died under the tanks and rain of bullets loosed upon them by the armies of the dictatorship.

§§§

Disaster could have been headed off, as late as the last week of April. Why did the government ignore the students' simple demands at a time when they easily could have met them? The students wanted only to have Hu Yaobang's case reconsidered, and to establish a dialogue with the government.

Changing the verdict on Hu would have cost nothing, since he was dead. It would have made the party look generous without surrendering any real power. Talking to the students, making some show of concern for them, understanding the popular will – these could have been done without giving up anything substantial.

Unfortunately, the party is never responsive to popular demands. Seeing itself as the repository of all truth, it never wants to indicate that spontaneous demonstrations can influence its policies.

Also, Premier Li Peng, once director of the State Education Commission, has contempt for the opinions of college students. He is used to treating them in a high-handed and contemptuous manner, regarding students as so many nuts and bolts to be wrenched into place to support the government's agenda.

He refused to respond to them at all until he was forced to talk to hunger strike leaders in the Great Hall of the People on May 18. It happened only after he decided to impose martial law on them, and then the confrontation infuriated him. By that time, the students had the support of the entire population of Beijing and were no longer in the mood to listen to cajolery or empty promises.

Li Peng and the conservatives did nothing to court popular support. Quite the contrary: they were continually enraging the populace. They acted in defense of power and privilege. Their maneuvers were a logical consequence of their politics.

General Secretary Zhao Ziyang tried to avert the disaster, but was stymied at every turn by the hard-liners. He and his intellectual supporters had spoken to the students in both conciliatory and encouraging ways, trying to win the support of the populace. This was the only rational chance they had to win the power struggle. He went all out in his drive for ultimate power until martial law was decided upon. Then he retreated without warning the students of their impending doom.

Because of his weakness, he too must bear some responsibility for the tragedy. Nevertheless, Zhao and the reforms he stood for represented the only hope that the party might have reconciled with the demonstrators.

When most of his older comrades remained intransigent against the students' demands for a posthumous rehabilitation of Hu Yaobang, Zhao spoke out in glowing terms about Hu's important contributions. Praise for Hu, now that he was dead, was tantamount to Zhao's praising his own political and economic orientation.

Then while the demonstrations were gaining critical mass, about April 23–30, Zhao went off on a scheduled trip to North Korea, leaving Premier Li Peng to handle this difficult situation. That meant Zhao was not present during a crucial meeting on April 24 in which the top leadership decided upon the inflammatory anti-student editorial that was published two days later in People's Daily, sparking the biggest demonstrations.

In retrospect, it is most unfortunate that Zhao Ziyang was not present at this discussion, to provide a moderating influence. If he had been, the anti-student editorial might have been toned down or headed off.

Premier Li claimed Zhao sent a telegram of support for the editorial from North Korea, and added that when he returned Zhao convened a meeting of the Politburo Standing Committee on May 1 in which he again supported it. If so, he changed his position in public one day later. Why?

Zhao made a special flight to the resort city of Beidaihe to meet with Deng. Deng supposedly said, "The most important thing for you (plural) to do is to stabilize the situation. As long as the situation can be stabilized, you need not worry about anything I said before. *If your plan works, we'll do it your way."*

Thinking he had Deng's support, Zhao returned to Beijing, where he made a public declaration on May 4 during a reception for officials of the Asian Bank. His statement, the "Ziyang Declaration," was hailed by most students, intellectuals and citizens of Beijing. He praised the students' patriotism, openly repudiated the editorial's definition of their movement as a disturbance, and called for the continued reform of the political system.

Some analysts argue that Zhao was acting on the advice of his closest political advisor, Bao Tong, who is currently under arrest. That may be so, but it seems unlikely he would have acted as he did if he didn't think he had Deng's support.

Zhao misjudged Deng. He watched the situation deteriorate in the hopes that the upheaval would discredit Li Peng, forcing Deng Xiaoping to hand over power to him. He dragged the Democracy Movement into his personal power play by publicly encouraging the students. Unfortunately for Zhao, his backers and the students, the old guard supported Li Peng as their proxy. In the showdown, when they believed their power was threatened by the mass movement, so did Deng Xiaoping. With their support, he backed Li Peng against Zhao Ziyang.

As soon as Deng decided to purge Zhao, both for his failure to subdue the demonstrations and for his public attacks on Deng himself, he had to turn to the old revolutionary veterans for support. After all, they had been criticizing Deng's handling of the student movement, and they had never favored the type of reform that Zhao represented.

The old comrades were allied with Premier Li Peng, Beijing Mayor Chen Xitong, and Beijing Party Secretary Li Ximing. As far as political and economic reforms are concerned, they were actually opponents of Deng's as well. They never liked opening China to what they consider the pollution of western ideas, and felt increasingly pressured by the changes that were taking place in the country over the past ten years. The old guard despised the well-known young intellectuals who repudiated China's "feudal tradition," rightly regarding it as an attack on their paternalistic despotism. If the demonstrations succeeded, they feared, they'd lose power and privilege.

And as revolutionaries, they weren't afraid to kill people in order to have their way.

They had always been there in the background, pushed back by

Deng through many hard-fought compromises, so that he could let younger men carry out his designs for China's economic development. The old comrades had been helpful in sacking Hu Yaobang in 1987, but at that time Deng still had Zhao to rely upon. Later, Zhao even became his "designated successor."

This time Deng needed their support because it was hard to convince many people under the age of 80 that Zhao was a criminal. In fact, a majority of the Central Committee members from provincial and city governments did not believe in Zhao's "counter-revolutionary" crimes. This was especially true of those from the coastal regions that benefited from Zhao's economic policies. Many of the highest military commanders were also reluctant to call Zhao a criminal.

The party never did brand Zhao as the ringleader of a "counter-revolutionary clique." Li Peng, Deng Xiaoping and their aged cronies weren't able to get majority support from the rest of the top leaders for such a radical move, which would amount to branding the General Secretary as a traitor.

Instead, they ordered the slaughter of students and young workers, later described as "the dregs of society." It ended the confrontation, established their absolute control, and frightened off political opposition from the people whose opinions carry weight in society.

Regional party leaders were summoned to Beijing for emergency meetings during the protests. They agreed with martial law, even went along with the idea that Zhao had made "serious mistakes" and deserved to be dismissed as General Secretary. But they would not subscribe to a public declaration that he was the leader of a "counter-revolutionary clique" attempting to overthrow the government.

Unable to convince the regional leadership to support them on the counter-revolutionary charge, Deng and company had to win over the commanders of China's seven military regions. The task was accomplished—though perhaps not completely—during the last week before the massacre. The details are secret, but the military hierarchy was apparently won over to the use of force only through personal face-to-face lobbying by Deng Xiaoping. Once the high command agreed in principle, it was only a matter of deciding which army should do the job.

Because President Yang Shangkun had close family connections with their officers, the 27th Army was chosen. Although many other military units were certainly involved in the massacre, the 27th is still believed to have done most of the killing.

The direct order to suppress the "rebellion" must have come from

Deng Xiaoping, but it's likely that Yang Shangkun further instructed the officers of his "family army" to kill as many people as they could. That would terrorize the Democracy Movement and at the same time prompt enough physical resistance to justify the purge that was already planned to follow.

Many western analysts believe Deng Xiaoping gave the orders for an assault, but that Yang dictated the scope and intensity of the violence. However, I talked with many knowledgeable Chinese after the massacre and not one of them thinks Deng was unaware of it. They all think he masterminded the whole thing.

According to them, it was in keeping with his character and natural inclinations. They reminded me that Deng was chiefly responsible for the level of violence used against intellectuals in the Anti-Rightist Campaign of 1957.

A contrary indication to this theory is that Chen Yizi, former chairman of the Committee for Restructuring the Economy, now in exile in France, said the decision to carry out a massacre was made by the hard-liners in the party leadership who had opposed Deng's reforms for the past ten years. It implies Deng may not have authorized the sort of wholesale bloodshed that took place. Nevertheless, I believe he did.

One reliable source now in the United States told me Deng issued an oral order for the troops to fire, but refused to sign a written order because he was worried about his name in history. He made President Yang sign it instead. Such a story appeared in the press in November.

§§§

The old revolutionary Deng Xiaoping had tried to do the impossible. He wanted to make China rich and powerful by introducing western technology, while not allowing the country to adopt the associated western ideas of freedom of democracy. His goal, in the words of the late nineteenth-century scholar Zhang Zhidong, was to "employ western learning as the function and Chinese learning as the substance" of reform.

Ironically for Deng, Chinese learning was encapsuled in his Four Cardinal Principles: socialism, dictatorship, the Communist Party and Marxism-Leninism-Mao Zedong Thought. Of the four, only dictatorship is traditionally Chinese.

Unfortunately for him, both of his hand-picked successors, Hu Yaobang and Zhao Ziyang, discovered that carrying out the changes he wanted and making the economy work required political reform at the top. They saw that the Four Cardinal Principles were so limited that in the end, the principles compromised his own stated policies of reform and openness.

The intellectual supporters of Hu and Zhao went further than they did. They continued to use these politicians as symbols of support for reform at the top, but they believed China needed a truly democratic political system. The majority of China's finest scholars, writers and other cultural leaders were aligned with this faction. They overwhelmingly supported the student movement, both before and after the declaration of martial law.

Deng Xiaoping was faced with a mass movement that had humiliated him at the moment of his greatest success – the summit with Mikhail Gorbachev. The demonstrators were demanding the removal of his premier and the posthumous rehabilitation of a disgraced general secretary. In the crisis, he certainly believed the government was in danger of being overthrown by a counter-revolutionary rebellion.

Rather than allow that, Deng did the only thing his generation of Chinese Communist leaders have ever known how to do in the face of strong opposition. Still fearful of his own people 40 years after the revolution, and devoid of any other way of enforcing his political authority, he decided to "shed a little blood."

As a result, China is in the midst of an upheaval unlike anything since the Cultural Revolution. The reforms Deng wanted are in grave jeopardy and the party itself is fragmented.

The Fourth Plenum of the party's Central Committee, at which the new Politburo was chosen, is an example of the way the rulers deal with the dissension that continues within the party. The session was held on June 23.

Most of the members of the Plenum were chosen in the fall of 1987, and they were much in favor of Zhao Ziyang's reforms. They had not been consulted about how to handle the Democracy Movement for fear that a majority would vote against the violent suppression wanted by the old guard.

For several weeks prior to this Plenum, many of the Central Committee members were given private "briefings" by the leadership. They were summoned to Beijing, housed in widely separated parts of town with armed soldiers guarding the gates, and held incommunicado. Many of the delegates, especially the intellectuals, disapproved of what had been done and didn't believe what they were told about a "counter-revolutionary rebellion."

Some had actually worked together against martial law before the massacre. Delegates from coastal provinces that had benefited most from Zhao's reforms were particularly opposed to stripping him of his official titles.

During the Plenum, a deputy commander of the 27th Army delivered a speech in which he explained "the current situation" to the delegates. He said no one who opposed Deng and the Communist Party leadership would escape the army's grasp, and this applied to all ranks, Politburo or Central Committee members, as well as "counter-revolutionary rebels." It was a clear threat.

The delegates were asked to support the new Politburo Standing Committee and the decision to strip Zhao Ziyang of all his offices. A delegate who declined to give his name told the editor of *Contention* magazine in Hong Kong, "The martial law troops forced us at gunpoint to raise our hands in approval."

An intense struggle for control of the army raged for six months after the massacre. Yang Shangkun and Deng Xiaoping were at odds over the powerful position of First Vice Chairman of the Central Military Commission. Yang wanted it for himself and Deng wanted either to abolish it or to pass it on to someone who remained committed to his economic reforms. Deng seemed to have won the first round by the appointment of a six- man group of generals and former generals, most believed to lean away from Yang's position, to share power with the First Vice Chairman. At the Fifth Plenum of the Central Committee on November 9, Deng Xiaoping announced his retirement as Chairman of the Central Military Commission and his replacement by his hand-picked successor and new General Secretary Jiang Zemin. With Deng's man installed as Chairman above him, Yang Shangkun was made First Vice Chairman. Yang's power was further shored up by the appointment of his brother, Yang Baibing, as General Secretary of the Central Military Commission. Although Jiang has the highest rank, most analysts agree that Yang Shangkun's position with the military is stronger. Thus the power struggle, the struggle for succession, continues with the question of military control only temporarily settled.

The new Politburo is weighted in favor of Stalinist-trained technocrats. They are attempting to re-establish the backward economic practices of the 1950s, and at the same time carry out a Cultural Revolution-style purge of the urban classes. If they succeed, they will compound China's already serious economic problems.

Their policies and the world's disgust with the massacre have already severely harmed the economy. In 1988, China had a deficit of $8 billion U.S., and it was higher in the first half of 1989 than the same time the previous year. The deficit was being financed by loans from the World Bank and other lender countries.

Reacting to the crackdown, the World Bank and many other institutions froze all loans to China. Commercial markets have dried up too, as potential investors look for safer places to make money.

The $2.2 billion U.S. tourism industry is gasping for breath and may not be revived for years. Millions of dollars per month are lost by keeping luxury hotels open, like the Shanghai Hilton and the Beijing International. American congressional representatives talk about linking progress in human rights to any future trade deals with China.

Add to these problems the government's inability to pay peasants hard currency for their summer harvests, and the imposition of new price controls. Both moves encourage the peasants to plant less grain and to slaughter their breeding animals. This creates a possibility of an urban food shortage.

In October the government announced that workers' salaries would be reduced by 30 to 60 percent across the board for the next few months. Workers are required to purchase three-year, interest-bearing bonds. The economic situation was reported as extremely grave in many widely separated areas of the country.

A friend recently showed me a letter sent from Shanghai, which gives an idea of the economy's distress. The writer notes that the government has been forcing people to buy state bonds—something the world press had already reported. But what we had not heard before was that for weeks the government also had been making citizens buy unwanted electrical appliances.

Even before the massacre, fans and refrigerators were being produced in greater quantities than required. Now that the economy was cooling rapidly and wages were dropping, there was even less demand.

So pressure is being applied in each work unit to make people buy these unwanted appliances under "bargain conditions." The customers agree to buy and pay for them now. The state-run enterprise promises that in five years they can bring in the receipt and get their money back. What a deal! You enjoy the use of the merchandise for five years without ever really paying for it. Many people were flocking to buy these commodities but, the letter added, "Everyone knows their money will not be forthcoming when the five years is up." It's just a new scheme to force people to lend money to the state.

Because of the economic slowdown, it seems probable that China's imports will be cut drastically and harsh financial restraints will be re-imposed.

§§§

The Stalinist repression and the reversal of economic reforms are the price exacted from Deng Xiaoping by the old revolutionaries for their support against Zhao and the students. But the conservatives face stiff opposition, both within the party and throughout the populace.

On August 30, the Standing Committee of the National People's Congress met to consider a list of nine serious crimes of Zhao Ziyang. The list was prepared by the Party Central Anti-Rebellion Committee, and the committee was asked to endorse the indictment.

Despite all the killing and threats, the Standing Committee sent it back for further study. It was an extraordinary show of independence. The committee voted 20 percent in favor of the indictment, 20 percent against, and 60 percent abstaining. This is a measure of the deep resistance to the leaders who were responsible for the massacre. It also helps explain why Deng, Li and Yang didn't call a meeting of this usually pliant body before the massacre.

How long can the present situation last? No one can say. China's government under this regime may lead to a number of different short-term scenarios. Only one of them appears certain. There will definitely be another major power struggle when Deng Xiaoping dies. This inevitability is not far off.

The current regime may remain in power for many years, controlling a dispirited populace with the army's support. High Communist Party and People's Liberation Army officers could continue to live well at the expense of the laboring masses and thus remain loyal to the regime. As long as they have the support of the army and the internal security apparatus, a very small ruling group can control the vast majority of the Chinese people almost indefinitely.

It seems more likely that a gradual economic decline will lead to increasing social strife which may take many different forms not all of which will be nonviolent. China might even experience complete economic collapse and a return to extreme regionalism.

In the event of such an economic decline, the current leadership group, facing widespread opposition to its regressive policies, will fall from power. Under what conditions this happens and what sort of regime comes after it will determine the prospects for continued democratization in China.

Perhaps the worst thing that could happen right after Deng's demise would be for President Yang Shangkun to gain the upper hand. He would create a ruthless military dictatorship more repressive than Deng's.

A more hopeful scenario is a return to the political and economic policies in practice before the massacre. This would require at least a partial repudiation of the massacre, similar to the partial repudiation of the Anti-Rightist Campaign in the late 1970s and early 1980s. Today's rulers would be blamed for letting a patriotic protest movement degenerate into a riot, and student and intellectual leaders would be rehabilitated, some of them posthumously. All of these things would perhaps maintain a semblance of party unity and win back the educated classes in the service of gradual economic and political reform. Such a return to the reform policies of the past ten years may be the best thing we can realistically hope to happen in China in what remains of this century. It would probably have to be accomplished either under a collective leadership, or more likely, under a newly emerged "strong man." The process would be similar to Deng Xiaoping's early backers repudiating the policies of the Cultural Revolution, in part to further their own careers.

Such a strong man will probably rise to the top in the course of the current succession struggle. He would not necessarily have the Chinese people's interests at heart any more than Deng Xiaoping did, but he would be a strong advocate of economic reform leading to "wealth and power."

This leads to another possibility, quite a bit less likely and more visionary, but not impossible: the emergence of a Chinese Gorbachev. He would have to embark on a genuine reform of the party apparatus and the economic system, enlisting the support of the intellectuals and the news media.

Such a leader would be welcomed by most of the urban population. He might come from the ranks of the so-called *taizi bang* (Gang of Imperial Heirs), children of high party officials said to be waiting in the background to take over when Li Peng and his transitional government are disposed of after the death of their powerful patrons. Many of them are now attending the finest American and European universities, and may be expected to support one of their own in the same way people of his generation and educational background now support Gorbachev. He would also have a greater chance of success than Gorbachev because China does not have a grave nationalities problem, except in Tibet and perhaps Xinjiang.

If events proceed in any of these hopeful ways, a new Chinese Constitution will eventually have to be written to accord with the actual political situation. To accomplish these goals will require a long and protracted struggle aimed at gradual liberalization of the current party-state system and of the economic and political sides of society. The ideas of the 1989 Democratic Movement and its now exiled and jailed leaders will play an important role if any of these hopeful changes take place after the death of the "old revolutionary comrades." Of course democracy cannot solve all of China's pressing economic and social problems, but it can ensure that the process of building a strong and livable society in China will take place under greater conditions of justice and fairness than has hitherto been the case in modern Chinese history.

In 1918, China's most celebrated writer, Lu Xun, was deeply depressed about the failure of the 1911 Revolution, which overthrew the last imperial dynasty but rapidly collapsed into dictatorship and civil war. Lu was approached by the editors of *New Youth* magazine to write stories for them. They wanted to awaken the Chinese people to the need for reform and the revolutionary transformation of the social, political and cultural system.

Lu Xun tried to turn them down but they persisted. Then out of his agony and despair, he invented the most memorable metaphor for China in the twentieth century: the iron house.

The passage, with which this book began, is well known to every beginning student of modern Chinese literature.

> Imagine an iron house without a single window and
> virtually indestructible, in which there are many
> people sleeping soundly. In a short time they will die of
> suffocation, but they will pass from slumber to
> annihilation without experiencing the sorrow of
> impending death. Now you shout loudly, waking up a
> few of the relatively light sleepers, causing these
> unfortunate few to suffer the agony of irrevocable
> death. Do you really think you have done them a
> good turn?

In Lu Xun's lifetime China was indeed such an iron house within which most of its then 400 million inhabitants were ignorant, impoverished, and unaware of the dangers surrounding them on every side. The masses were "sleeping soundly" and the intellectuals were the "unfortunate few" who anticipated with unbearable agony the impending annihilation of their rapidly disintegrating homeland.

After 30 years of invasion and civil war, the victorious Communist Party established a unified nation with a new name and a new ideology. During another 30 tortuous years, some impressive gains were made, but most of them were offset by a deliberately uncontrolled population explosion and numerous destructive mass campaigns.

The human significance of those material gains was nullified by the spiritual price the Chinese people were forced to pay for them. During that period, not only was China's iron house not destroyed, but under the party's dictatorship it became even more oppressive and suffocating in every area of civil life. China's windows to the world were welded over with iron shutters and the doors were riveted shut.

Then, late in 1976, the leaders of the Cultural Revolution were thrown into prison, where they remain. Two years later, Deng Xiaoping and his supporters "shouted out loudly" that the doors and windows of the iron house should be opened—and they were, as they never had been since the 1920s.

This time not only "a few of the relatively light sleepers" were awakened, but throughout Chinese society, from the peasantry to the Politburo, the social, political, and cultural consciousness of the Chinese people began to be transformed. They began to build a more spacious mansion containing many different rooms where people practiced the multiform arts of modern living.

Unfortunately, the other old men who had ruled China for so many years, before Deng purchased their reluctant retirement, were unhappy with the new mansion that was taking shape. Its polyphonic sounds, polymorphic shapes and variegated color schemes were painful to their ears and eyes. It no longer resembled the iron house in which they felt at ease. It was no longer their home. They were losing control of its inhabitants.

On April 24, 1989, appalled at the inevitable results of his own rebuilding, Deng Xiaoping made a pact with his old comrade-enemies. The pact was sealed with the blood of children on June 3 and 4, under the "Gate of Heavenly Peace."

Now these old men have assigned cadre work crews to every corner of the half-built mansion. Their instructions are to weld and rivet iron plates over the doors and windows—to rebuild the iron house.

But the rips and tears in the iron house reach from the basement to the rooftop. And the cadres are loath to do the work assigned them. Even they have grown accustomed to the newly glimpsed rainbows of light that lately shone prismatically into their cave. They procrastinate; they malinger; and they wait for the change of orders that always follows an imperial funeral. They do not wish to join the unfortunate many this time and experience "the agony of irrevocable death" by suffocation. They question Deng Xiaoping: "Do you think you have done us a good turn?"

Some of my friends whose words fill these pages are in prison. Others are in exile in Europe and America. Some still dwell in the iron house. Most of them live in frustration, anger, and fear, waiting for a knock on the door in the middle of the night. They too wait for an imperial death and shudder to think what may come after. All around them iron gates are closing, computer networks are shutting down, phone lines are being tapped.

Perhaps some of them remember what Lu Xun's friend Qian Xuantong said in answer to his pessimistic parable of the iron house: "But if a few of them have already awakened, you cannot say there is absolutely no hope of destroying the iron house."

What remains of the iron house suffers from metal fatigue. Many more than a few of its inhabitants have long ago awakened from their slumber. Perhaps they will not allow themselves to be chained up again. Perhaps the geriatric architects of iron and steel cannot repair the rents and tears in the sides of the iron house. Perhaps the iron house has already been transformed too far beyond recognition. Perhaps the old blueprints have been lost. Perhaps.

A CALL TO ACTION

F OR MANY, IT IS FRUSTRATING TO READ OF THE EVENTS IN China and feel helpless. Yet much has been done and can still be done by individuals, working either on their own or with other organizations. As soon as the events of the Chinese Democracy Movement became known, a number of groups and organizations began to work on a variety of fronts. Human rights organizations, legal aid societies, trade groups, student organizations, and others quickly moved to alert the world and to put Chinese authorities on notice that the abuse of students and citizens would not go unnoticed. These groups' activities are varied and reflect their particular missions. In an effort to provide a forum for these groups, the publisher extended invitations to several to explain their organizations and their involvement in the events in China. The information is the very latest at press time. More specifics can be had by contacting the groups directly.

AMNESTY INTERNATIONAL USA

Amnesty International (AI), the Nobel Peace Prize-winning human rights organization, responded immediately by launching a worldwide letter-writing campaign aimed at national, provincial, and municipal authorities in China. Many hundreds of the letters were copied and sent to the Chinese Embassy and office of the China News Agency. AI also set up a toll-free number which allowed thousands of people to send telegrams to Chinese officials.

Amnesty International realizes that its role is even more critical now and that action is even more essential than in the days immediately following the Tiananmen massacre. The story of the gross human rights violations has slipped from the front page of international concern, the outcry has become muted. Yet according to AI's records, at least 200 people have been executed after summary trials. Over 2000 have been detained and scores of arrests take place every day. Trials have not conformed to international standards as guilt is assumed by the court.

AI's current priorities are:

- prevent further executions
- seek the release of those arrested for exercising their basic rights
- prevent further arrests

Amnesty International jealously guards its impartiality and independence. It supports no particular government, advocates no form of government. It does not call for sanctions or economic boycotts. Keeping these points in mind, they suggest the following two **immediate** actions for readers:

Action #1

Send telegrams and express letters to Chinese government officials listed below:

- expressing concern that those arrested have been charged with an offense punishable by death and may be tried according to procedures which fall far short of international standards for fair trials (Amnesty International opposes **all** uses of the death penalty as a violation of the right to life as enshrined in the United Nations' Universal Declaration of Human Rights.)

- urging the authorities to ensure that those arrested are afforded all facilities for a fair trial before an independent, competent, and impartial tribunal, in accordance with internationally agreed standards, and to ensure if convicted they will not be executed.

- asking the officials to make public a full record of all such trials, including the procedures followed and the evidence against the accused

Appeals should be sent to:

Li Peng
Prime Minister
Prime Minister's Office
Beijing
People's Republic of China

Liu Fuzhi Jianchazhang
Supreme Chief Procurator
Zuigao Renmin Jianchayuan
Beijingshi

People's Republic of China
Copies should be sent to:
  Ambassador Zhu Qizhen
  Embassy of the People's Republic of China
  2300 Connecticut Ave. NW
  Washington, DC 20008

Action #2

An 800 number has been set up to enable concerned parties to directly send telegrams to Chinese officials. The China Emergency Action Toll Free Telegraph Number is 1-800-888-5284. Please distribute this number as widely as possible.

Contact information

For more information regarding Amnesty International's work on China, contact:
  Amnesty International
  National Campaign Office
  655 Sutter #406
  San Francisco, CA 94102
  (415) 441-2114

If you are interested in joining an AI group in your community or the national organization, write:
  Amnesty International USA
  322 Eighth Ave.
  New York, NY 10001
  (212) 807-8400

The international office can be reached at:
  Amnesty International
  1 Easton St.
  London WC1X 8DJ
  England

ASIA WATCH

Asia Watch is one of several groups under the umbrella organization Human Rights Watch. Coincidentally, Asia Watch China specialist Robin Munro was also one of the few foreigners to witness the events of June 3-4. China Watch mounted an emergency effort by setting up a network for receiving information, trying to distinguish fact from rumor, pressing Congress and the Bush Administration for an appropriate response, and working to protect individuals in danger.

The main sources for correct information were the official Chinese media and the Chinese student network in the United States. For the first few weeks, provincial radio stations and national and local newspapers throughout China announced the names of those arrested. The information was picked up by the Hong Kong press and the wire services. Chinese students, communicating with each other by computer, learned of friends who had been arrested. Robin Munro began a careful compilation of eyewitness accounts of the events on Tiananmen Square.

Asia Watch ran a full-page ad in *The New York Times* on June 25 announcing its documentation effort and listing several cases. More information flooded in. A fax system was set up to keep interested parties informed on a daily basis – first a few contacts and then a myriad of human rights organizations and China specialists in the U.S., Canada, Europe, and Hong Kong.

Armed with articles from the U.S. Chinese-language press and fax directories for China, the organization began feeding faxes on the killings and arrests directly into China, keeping it up until the machines were unplugged on the receiving end.

Asia Watch also worked out a program with a number of donors to get emergency financial assistance and academic placements for stranded Chinese nationals and acted as a referral agency for people needing advice on visas and asylum. To facilitate this and other related work, Asia Watch has established an office in Hong Kong, where current information can be more readily collected.

Contact Information

For more information about the work of this important human rights organization, contact:

Asia Watch
485 Fifth Ave.
New York, NY   10017
(212) 972-8400
(212) 972-0905 (fax)

ASSOCIATION OF OVERSEAS HONG KONG CHINESE FOR DEMOCRACY AND HUMAN RIGHTS (AOHKCDHR)

The AOHKCDHR was founded about two weeks after the Tiananmen massacre. The membership is primarily composed of students and professionals in the Boston area. Most student members are from

Boston University, Brandeis, Brown, Harvard, MIT, Northeastern, Framingham State College, and Museum of Fine Arts Institute.

Objectives of the organization are:

- to promote democracy and human rights in China and Hong Kong
- to inform members about the most recent developments in China and Hong Kong
- to create a forum and network for members to exchange views on the future of China and Hong Kong

AOHKCDHR activities since the massacre have included (1) fund raising campaigns for The May 4 Foundation, China Relief Fund, and Hong Kong Red Cross, (2) petition campaign (gathered 10,000 signatures) to President Bush and the Senate asking for stronger action, (3) lobbying congress for the Dixon/Pelosi Bill, (4) discussion forums and lectures, and (5) a 100th-Day Memorial. In addition, AOHKCDHR distributes video tapes of events in China and publishes a newsletter in English and Chinese every 2–3 weeks.

Contact information

Association of Overseas Hong Kong Chinese for Democracy and Human Rights
P.O. Box 259, MIT Branch
Cambridge, MA 02139

CHINA INFORMATION CENTER

During the early days of the Tiananmen Square demonstrations, Chinese students throughout the Boston area organized the China Information Center. The Center rapidly emerged as a communications hub for Chinese students nationwide who wished to support their fellow students in Beijing.

The China Information Center was the only organization to have a direct "hot line" to Tiananmen Square, receiving constant reports and updates on the events as they transpired. All information received by the Center in those days was exclusive and immediate. When the Western media was silenced and sent home by the Chinese government, the Center became the media's main source of up-to-the-minute information.

After the massacre, the Center communicated the details of the events via fax and telephone to those in China who could not rely on the information presented by the government-controlled media. As long as phone lines remained open, the Center continued to pass on news reports and photographs and to respond to the inquiries of Chinese citizens calling for the truth.

Because of the severity of the government's crackdown, it has become increasingly difficult and dangerous to communicate with individuals in China. Fear of government reprisal has coerced the citizens of China into an unwilling silence. Despite this, efforts at communication continue.

The China Information Center believes that openness and the flow of information are the basic and defining characteristics of a humanitarian society. Based on that belief, the organization has set the following tasks for itself in the future:

- to continue providing up-to-date information to the press and general public regarding developments in China
- to create a human rights archive, storing information regarding arrests and executions as well as a record of all Chinese citizens killed in the massacre. In this effort, the Center works with Amnesty International and Asia Watch. The archive also seeks to store records and materials related to China's pro-democracy movement
- to support the efforts of other Chinese who are working to provide news of current developments in China, including a newspaper by Chinese students in exile and daily Chinese language radio broadcasts that penetrate China
- to publish a monthly newsletter in English, documenting their work and continuing the flow of information about China
- to conduct research focusing on political, military, legal, and business-related topics
- to provide a communications network for Chinese students in the U.S. and abroad who are unable to return to their homeland, and to provide financial assistance to Chinese students to conduct nationwide teleconferences
- to help increase the academic community's awareness (through conferences and seminars) of the contemporary political, economic, and social changes in China and the potential impact of these changes on future China-U.S. relations.

One of the most important activities of the Center is the publication of a comprehensive list of Chinese student organizations in the U.S.

Contact information

China Information Center
169 Grove St.

Newton, MA 02166
(617) 332-0990
(617) 332-2638 (fax)

VANCOUVER SOCIETY IN SUPPORT OF DEMOCRATIC MOVEMENT

The Vancouver Society in Support of Democratic Movement is an organization dedicated to keeping alive the memory of the events of the pro-democracy movement and subsequent government destruction of the peaceful movement. The Society has organized several memorial services, marches, and peaceful demonstrations to protest the government's actions and to call for a stop to all political repercussions and summary executions upon arrest. One such rally drew a crowd of over 10,000.

During the first days after the government crackdown the Society participated in the effort to fax news and information directly to China. They also launched a campaign to jam the China reporting hot line to delay the arrest of students and citizens in China. They started a project to build their own Goddess of Democracy, produced an information booklet and a commemorative T-shirt, held a sympathy fast and built a tent city, and undertook other such activities.

The Society encourages anyone concerned with the current critical situation in China, anyone who might have information or videos or photographs of the events, or who would like to continue to work in some way to get in touch with them.

Contact information

Vancouver Society in Support of Democratic Movement
427 Dunlevy St. #202
Vancouver, BC V6A 3Y4
Canada
(604) 669-6938
(604) 986-4716 (fax)

JUNE 4TH CHINA SUPPORT

A London-based group closely linked with China through its members' work, study, trade, and friendship, the group acts to:

- provide counseling to any Chinese nationals in Britain and any refugees escaping from China who may need to prolong their stay abroad due to the events there

• gather information on the events leading up to and following the June 4 attack on the students and to promote a well-documented and balanced view of these events and their significance

• monitor the detention, arrests, sentencing, or execution of any individual due to involvement in the events in China, and then to disseminate the information to all relevant parties

• inform the government and people of Britain about the significance of the events of the pro-democracy movement for the future of Hong Kong and China and to lobby the government on issues arising from the events

June 4th China Support is primarily a volunteer organization that raises money for its activities through various appeals. They produce a newsletter periodically giving details of the group's activities. The monitoring group produces an alphabetical list of all named individuals who have been arrested to date, with brief biographical notes and information on date and place of arrest where available. Lists broken down by profession and by city or province are also available upon request.

The counseling group advises Chinese nationals in Britain on questions concerning visa extensions, work permits, obtaining accommodation, and social security relief. A portion of the money raised by the organization is used to offer financial assistance to Chinese nationals forced to prolong their stay in Britain because of the recent events. The group has also rented a flat to house refugees and assists them in other areas, offering counseling, advice, practical help, and support.

June 4th China Support is helping to organize a collection of documents, photographs, and audio and video tapes on the events surrounding June 4, which will be cataloged and made available for research.

The organization has been very active in arranging public events in conjunction with other groups to provide a balanced view of the conflict in China and to keep alive the memory of what happened. So far these events have included the erection of a replica of the Goddess of Democracy outside the Chinese Embassy in London, a China Appeal Day complete with speeches by Wuer Kaixi and others and an exhibition, a flower-laying mourning ceremony in London's Chinatown followed by an evening vigil outside the Chinese Embassy, and a rally in London's Chinatown and march to the embassy. Spring activities include an April 1990 art exhibition and sale in London, assisted by Christie's, where works of art donated by individuals and organizations will be sold. Dame Elizabeth Frink and Robert Rauschenberg are among the many artists represented.

The monitoring group, in liaison with other monitoring organizations both in the U.K. and abroad, produced a list of 398 named individuals who had been arrested by August 1989 in connection with the June 4th events. This list was mailed to human rights organizations and interested people. Further lists are produced periodically. This information has also been used for a portable traveling exhibition that is shown at relevant events throughout the U.K.

The lobbying group writes to and meets with members of the British government with regard to residence status of Chinese nationals while the present conditions prevail in China.

Contact information

June 4th China Support
152 Camden High St.
London NW1 ONE
England
(01) 485-8236
(01) 281-3230 (fax)

SOURCES AND ACKNOWLEDGMENTS

ALL OF THE STATEMENTS RECORDED HERE AS BEING made to me by Chinese citizens are reported accurately, but I have used their real names only when their words or actions are a matter of public record. For the rest, details of time and place as well as the names, sexes, and occupations of my friends and informants have been fictionalized in order to protect them from the revenge of the Chinese government and security apparatus. For convenience I have employed the masculine pronoun, regardless of the person's gender, when referring to people who must remain anonymous.

The account I have given of mass killings on Tiananmen Square itself, especially on the north side of the Monument to the Revolutionary Martyrs, faithfully reproduces evidence offered by Chinese eyewitnesses. I know that my report contradicts the official Chinese government version of events. It also contradicts the *New York Times* bureau chief Nicholas Kristof's categorical statement that there was "no massacre in Tiananmen Square." (*New York Times Magazine*, November 12, 1989, p. 71.) Kristof offers no evidence for his statement except that he did not personally witness such a massacre. I have no qualms about rejecting his views. He, like myself, was not on the square at the time in question. Robin Munro, an Asia Watch China specialist, has also written (in *Human Rights Watch* No. 3, September 1989) that he does not believe there was a massacre on the square itself. He and another reporter were on the square and under the monument from 2:00 until 5:20 A.M. when they joined a crowd as it retreated toward the southeast off the monument with "no sign of panic there, not the slightest evidence of any massacre having just occurred."

His statement is in direct contradiction with several very detailed reports of events between 2:30 and 5:30 A.M. They include those of a Qinghua University student, a Beijing Institute of Chemical Engineering student, a student from outside Beijing I've dubbed Hua, and the pseudonymous Mr. Wang, as well as an anonymous Beijing news reporter who gave a press conference at the Lidu Hotel on June 5. The first three of these eyewitnesses agree on four things that happened on the square: troops shot the student loudspeaker down off the Monument to the Revolutionary Martyrs; troops fired into the air; police and troops used clubs to beat students on the square, injuring and bloodying many of them; students ran in panic from the beating and the shooting behind them, many falling and being trampled. The Qinghua and Chemical Engineering students agree that the tanks ran over people on the square; Hua and the Qinghua student report seeing troops fire directly into rows of unresisting students; Hua and Chai Ling (not quoted in my text) assert that tanks ran over tents with people still alive in them.

Munro's report of no panic at all even contradicts the statement of Hou Dejian (still resident in Beijing and subject to the authorities there). He reported seeing tanks on the square while people covered with blood were being rushed off beside one of them, troops firing at the loudspeaker on the monument, and himself being knocked to the ground and nearly trampled upon by students and others running away from the troops who were beating them from behind with clubs. As this book goes to press, Li Lu, deputy commander under Chai Ling of the student demonstration on Tiananmen Square, published an article entitled "In China, I'd Be Dead and Bush Wouldn't Care" on the editorial page of the *New York Times* for Sunday, December 24, 1989. He wrote in part: "I understand Mr. Bush's desire to believe the Chinese government. I wanted to believe the promise of safe passage my Government gave in the predawn hours of June 4. As I led 3,000 students out of Tiananmen Square, tanks opened fire and crushed students who were too exhausted to leave their tents. I will never forget the dark horror of the morning."

How are we to explain these inconsistencies without accusing either the Chinese eyewitnesses or Mr. Munro of deliberate fabrication? Thinking back to my time spent on the square, to the great distances involved and the difficulty of seeing from one spot on the square to another *in the clear light of day*, especially to the impossibility of seeing what might be going on on the north side of the Monument to the Revolutionary Martyrs from a vantage point on the south or southeast or southwest side of it (the three- tiered pedestal of the monument is as high as a small house and considerably wider), I believe that Munro saw what he saw, but there is no way he could have seen all. I continue to believe that the Chinese eyewitness reports are basically true, although some details of time, place, or numbers of dead and wounded may be slightly off. What I can not believe is that all of these Chinese people who risked their lives to speak to journalists and to smuggle out evidence of the massacre (several such eyewitnesses were subsequently arrested) and who had no private contact with each other after the events, could have collectively fabricated stories that agree in as many details as their do. Many other eyewitness reports and photographs remain hidden in China. The whole truth of the massacre will not be known until it is repudiated by a future Chinese government and the participants on both sides, those firing the guns and those fired upon, are free to tell their complete stories.

In the interests of truth I have tried to determine what actually happened on Tiananmen Square that night. When I contacted many exiled Chinese informants, all of whom believe there was killing on the square, they expressed great distress at the response of some Western governments and journalists. Whether there were killings on the square itself or not, they reason, there was clearly a massacre of a peacefully demonstrating civilian population carried out by a government that is currently engaged in the brutal suppression of human rights in China. I believe that Li Lu asks a valid question in his article: "Why is China an exception?" Why do the Western democracies and Japan continue to materially support the cruel dictatorship in China while opposing it with lofty rhetoric in the cases of Europe and Latin America?

§§§

I have many people to thank for this book. First and most importantly, the people of Beijing, from intellectual leaders to ordinary townspeople, who so generously shared their thoughts and feelings with a foreign stranger. The Academy of Sciences for sending me to China, and the staff of the Committee for Scholarly Communication with the People's Republic of China for retrieving my personal belongings, including seventeen tape recordings made at Peking University and Tiananmen Square. Many Chinese friends living abroad whose names I will not reveal. Mr. and Mrs. Lam Shan-muk, publishers of the *Hongkong Economic Journal,* for encouraging me to write up my diary, of which they published an abbreviated Chinese version in July and August 1989. Professor Terry McGee of the University of British Columbia Institute of Asian Research and Raymond Chan of the Vancouver Society in Support of the Democratic Movement for providing me two forums to express my views in public. Professor Lin Yü-sheng for sending me his published reflections on the Democracy Movement and Chinese Society. Mr. and Mrs. Xu Xing for furnishing me with dozens of eyewitness reports of the massacre collected from Hong Kong journals. Chen Jo-hsi, author of *The Execution of Mayor Yin*, for giving me her published reports on the massacre. Professors Marsha Wagner, Joseph S. M. Lau, and Howard Goldblatt for stimulating discussions at the University of Colorado where Goldblatt was our host for a two-day conference. Professor Ralph W. Huenemann, Director of the University of Victoria Centre for Asia-Pacific Initiatives, for information on the Chinese economy. Rene Goldman for providing eyewitness reports published in Paris. Joseph M. Bauman Jr. of Salt Lake City for his invaluable expert editorial assistance in preparing my original manuscript for popular publication. Chiu Weiwei (my sister-in- law) for sending me important information on the massacre from Taiwan. And my wife, Josephine Chiu-Duke, for reading through a mountain of Chinese newspapers and journals, selecting those items most important to an understanding of the situation in China, translating my translation of the diary into proper Chinese, reading the manuscript through several times, and providing innumerable helpful ideas and suggestions, which contributed greatly to the value of the book. Without her help the book simply could not have been written. I am totally responsible for whatever inevitable errors of fact may be discovered in this narrative. The overall interpretation of events is also my own responsibility.

In Chapter 2, I have benefited from three books for the discussion of democracy movements from 1979 to 1987: Andrew J. Nathan's *Chinese Democracy* (New York: Alfred A. Knopf, 1985), Editor James D. Seymour's *The Fifth Modernization: China's Human Rights Movement, 1978-1979* (Stanfordville, NY: Human Rights Publishing Group, 1980), and Orville Schell's *Discos and Democracy: China in the Throes of Reform* (New York: Pantheon Books, 1988). The 1978-79 quotations are from Nathan; Wei Jingsheng quotations are from Seymour; Fang Lizhi quotations are from Schell.

In addition to seventeen hours of materials personally recorded in Beijing, I have also relied on the following sources, listed here in alphabetical order.

Chinese Journals

Asia Weekly (Yazhou zhoukan, Hong Kong)
Bai Xing (Hong Kong)
China Times Weekly (Shibao zhoukan, Taibei)
Contention (Zhengming, Hong Kong)

Mingbao Monthly (Hong Kong)
Mirror Monthly (Jingbao yuekan, Hong Kong)
The Ninties (Jiushi niandai, Hong Kong)

Chinese Newspapers

China Times (Zhongguo shibao, Taibei)
Far East Daily (Dongfang ribao, Hong Kong)
Free Times (Ziyou shibao)
Guangming Daily (Beijing)
Hongkong Economic Journal (Xin bao)
International Daily News (Guoji ribao, North American edition)
Mingbao Daily News (Hong Kong)
People's Daily (Renmin ribao, Beijing)
Sing Tao Daily News (Xingdao ribao, Vancouver edition)
United Daily (Lianhe bao, Taibei)
Wenhuibao (Hong Kong, PRC publication)
The World Journal (Shijie ribao, Vancouver edition)

Special Chinese Publications

An Authentic Record of Bloodstained China (Xuexi Zhonghua shilu, Hong Kong: *Wenhuibao*, June 13, 1989)

Fifty Days of the Beijing Student Movement (Beijing xueyun wushi ri, Taibei: *China Times*, June 20, 1989)

A Historical Record (Lishi de cunzheng, Taibei, Center for the Study of Mainland China Problems, August 1, 1989)

English Periodicals

American Photographer (September 1989)
Asia Watch Reports
Asiaweek
China Daily (Beijing publication)
Far Eastern Economic Review
Newsweek
New York Review of Books
New York Times
New York Times Magazine
Paris Match (June 15, 1989, my one French journal)
TIME
Vanity Fair (October 1989)
The World & I (October 1989)

My account of the Tiananmen Massacre is based on many more eyewitness accounts than those actually quoted. I have used the following sources:

The Beijing Institute of Chemical Engineering student's remarks were reported by Yu Wen in *Bai Xing* (June 16, 1989): 22-23.

The anonymous Beijing newsman's statement was recorded by Xia Fen in *Bai Xing* (July 1, 1989): 9-12.

Chai Ling (General Director of the Tiananmen Directorate), "Republic, You Must Remember Well, These Children Were Fighting For You!" [Gongheguo, ni yao jizhu, zhe shi wei ni fendou de haizi!] *Hongkong Economic Journal* (June 14, 1989): 1. This is a printed version of a videotaped statement smuggled out of China. It appeared in many other publications.

Cheng Ying, "From Encirclement to Massacre" [Cong weicheng dao tusha], *The Ninties* (June 16, 1989): 12-18.

Hou Dejian's report, written in the Australian Embassy in Beijing, published in *World Journal* (August 24 and 25, 1989): 10.

Pierre Hurel, "Dans la Nuit Sanglante de Pekin," *Paris Match* (June 15, 1989): 75-76.

The Waidi student's report appeared in *World Journal* (June 24, 1989): 21. It was recorded from Hong Kong radio. In the manuscript he has been given the pseudonym Hua, meaning "a Chinese."

Wenhuibao's An Authentic Record of Bloodstained China: 1-11 and 40-55.

Xiao Zhang's statement was reported in *You Fang*, "Hou Dejian and Xiao Zhang" [Hou Dejian he Xiao Zhang], *Mingbao Monthly* (August 1989): 43-44.

Mrs. Li's report was given in Chen Jo-hsi's "A Death for a Death!" [Sike? Beijing ren kesi!] *Free Times* (June 6, 1989): 15. The article also appeared in the *Overseas Chinese Daily* (June 17) and *Hongkong Economic Journal* (June 20).

Yan Zhun was quoted in *World Journal* (September 18–22): 10.

The Qing Hua University student was quoted in *Wenhuibao's An Authentic Reocrd of Bloodstained China*: 56-64.

Li Dan's words are from *Bai Xing* (July 16, 1989): 10-11.

Xin Ku's remarks on Liu Xiaopo are from *World Journal* (October 3, 1989): 10.

Yue Wu's statements were quoted in *World Journal* (August 25, 1989): 20.

Estimates of casualties are from *Contention* (July 1989): 10.

Deng Xiaoping's opinions are given in Sun Shixian, "Deng Xiaoping zhenya xueyun de qianyin houguo" [The Causes and Effects of Deng Xiaoping's Suppression of the Student Movement], *World Journal* (July 12, 1989): 21. This article was originally published in Hong

Kong's *Mirror Monthly* (July 1989). It contains lengthy summaries of conversations between Deng Xiaoping, Li Peng, and Yang Shangkun at Deng's home on April 24 and is obviously based upon information supplied by some high-level Chinese Communist Party functionary. The complete text of Deng Xiaoping's June 9 congratulatory speech to the martial-law troops is in *World Journal* (June 21, 1989): 21. An English translation distributed by Xinhuashe is in the *New York Times* (June 30, 1989): A4.

THE IRON HOUSE

Designed by J. Scott Knudsen

Layout used Ventura Publisher

Composed by The Type Connection in Goudy Oldstyle
with display lines in ITC Grizzly

Printed by Publishers Press on Simpson Satin-Kote,
60 lb. ecru book;
cover paper is Speckletone French,
80 lb. cream cover.

Bound by Mountain States Bindery